Letters from London

Letters from London
Seven essays by
C.L.R. James

Edited by Nicholas Laughlin
With an introduction by Kenneth Ramchand

PROSPECT PRESS

Distributed in North America by the University Press of New England

First published in book form in 2003 by Prospect Press
(an imprint of Media & Editorial Projects (MEP) Ltd.)
6 Prospect Avenue
Maraval
Port of Spain
Trinidad and Tobago
www.readcaribbean.com

ISBN 976-95057-5-7 (hardcover)
ISBN 976-95057-4-9 (paperback)

Published in the United Kingdom in 2003 by Signal Books
36 Minster Road
Oxford OX4 1LY
United Kingdom
www.signalbooks.co.uk

ISBN 1-902669-60-6 (hardcover)
ISBN 1-902669-61-4 (paperback)

Distributed in North America
by the University Press of New England
1 Court Street, Ste 250
Lebanon
New Hampshire 03766
USA
www.upne.com

Cover and book design by Illya Furlonge-Walker,
Form and Function Design, Trinidad and Tobago

Printed in Trinidad and Tobago
by Caribbean Paper & Printed Products (1993) Ltd.

Contents

Introduction   ix

Editorial Note   xxx

Letters from London

A Visit to the Science and Art Museums   1

The Bloomsbury Atmosphere   17

Bloomsbury Again   37

The Houses   57

The Men   73

The Women   91

The Nucleus of a Great Civilisation   109

Notes   126

Index   140

Introduction

By Kenneth Ramchand,
Professor Emeritus of West Indian Literature,
University of the West Indies, St. Augustine, Trinidad

About Britain, I was a strange compound of knowledge and ignorance.

Beyond a Boundary, *1963*

The essays in this volume were written by C.L.R. James almost immediately upon his arrival in the United Kingdom in 1932. They allow us to observe an assertive Trinidadian outsider trying to combine what he is now finding out for himself about England and the English with what he thinks he already knows, as an insider created by a sound colonial education.

But the essays are also significant for showing us a James who is at ease in England, confident about his intellectual superiority, and apparently able to live comfortably with a quota of discrepant attitudes and interests. Look at how he ends a two-part essay on the intellectual atmosphere of the Bloomsbury district, the student and young writers' quarter that included the University of London and the British Museum: "Even though I see the Bloomsbury life for the secondary thing that it is, nevertheless both by instinct and by training I belong to it and have fit into it as naturally as a pencil fits into a sharpener. Birds of a feather will flock together." The diverse elements poised in James's constitution in 1932 are to be a source of internal conflict later, when his political and social consciousness is more strictly and technically developed. Since he is a good observer, some of the things he notices in 1932 turn out to be of critical importance in his evolving vision of politics, society and the individual.

These seven essays are selected from nine articles published in the *Port of Spain Gazette* in 1932. The *Gazette's* editor and publisher at this time was Andre P.T. Ambard. No details have been found so far, but James must have made an arrangement with the newspaper before he left Trinidad, testimony to his status as an acknowledged voice in his society. The first of the nine articles, "Barbados and Barbadians", (not included in this volume) was published in two instalments on 20 and 22 March, 1932. The ninth, "Proconsuls Beware: a cautionary tale" (also not included in this volume), was published on 11 September.

All the essays included here begin with the characteristic Jamesian declaration of what he is about to say, how he is going to say it, and what limitations there are to his presentation. Most of them end with a conclusion or a recapitulation. In all of them there is a forceful rationality, in all of them there is a strong sense of a sophisticated speaking voice. But something is missing. James writes with enthusiasm but not with the unwatched enthusiasm of youth. More often than not there is a distance between himself and what he is saying, as if he is looking on at his own performance. The reader is struck as much by the lack of intimacy and real companionship as by the thought that James does not notice this lack.

Is it significant that he doesn't give the names of any of his associates? Who is the twenty-one-year-old West African "who reads a volume of Proust at a sitting and reads Descartes, Berkeley and Spinoza in order to train his mind"? Which friend wrote the brilliant story that will make many laugh some day? What was the name of the poet, short story writer and magnificent baritone who read and sang to him as he lay in bed after a long night of intellectual talk on the floor before the fire with his platonic girl-friend?

The seven essays follow one another in a logical sequence. In the first, the newly-arrived James is being the tourist, visiting the places he has enjoyed in books; he goes up and down checking out art galleries, museums and libraries, looking at first editions, photographs, statues and busts, giving faces and bodies to personages he has met many times in imagination. In "A Visit to the Science and Art Museums", we see the ever-curious and appreciative James teaching himself about some major scientific moments and monuments, and wondering why there cannot be something like this museum in his own country. A brilliant description in this essay of a clock preserved from the fourteenth century can be seen as a comment on the narrow peaceable life of people and cultures (like the English, the reader finds himself thinking) that play it safe and regulate their excitements:

> There was an old clock from Wells Cathedral which was working before the end of the fourteenth century. In the middle of the last century new works were installed and the clock was removed to the Museum. . . . I had a good look at that old clock. Rather a dull existence tick-ticking away, with a little recurrent

excitement every quarter of an hour. But I couldn't help remembering with envy that in a few years I would probably be gone, while the old beast would probably be there in a thousand years, tick-ticking away, living his narrow but peaceable life.

After convincing us that he is convinced of the necessity of the Science Museum, the sense of mortality playfully expressed in his comments on the clock is awakened by the sight of Rodin's *John the Baptist* in the Victoria and Albert Museum. James thinks of it as "a naked man walking". If a wanderer from the West Indies three thousand years from now were to see today's exhibits in the Science Museum, he would see them as obsolete designs and meaningless models. "But in the Art Museum he will see the statue of the man walking. It will be to him as it is to me. It cannot grow old. It cannot go out of date. It is timeless, made materially of bronze but actually, as has been said of great literature, the precious life-blood of a master spirit." At the end of this 1932 essay, then, the James that cannot go out of date affirms the conviction of the necessity and immortality of art. As he develops, he seeks to integrate this conviction into all his doing and thinking, and to install it as a humbling and ennobling perspective on all human endeavour.

In the next two essays he writes about the Bloomsbury atmosphere, and you get the feeling that, at the age of thirty-one, this self-educated man with a professorial reputation is living at last, in five hectic days and nights, the life of the intellectually thirsty undergraduate he had never allowed himself to be when he refused to study for the Island

Scholarship at Queen's Royal College (Q.R.C.) in Trinidad. He found these activities distinctive, and "so absolutely different from life in the West Indies that it stands out as easily the most striking of my first impressions." Was it really any more elevating than the doings of the group of writers, artists, musicians and political people, sometimes called the *Beacon* group, to which James had belonged at home?

Essays four, five and six deal respectively with the houses and rooms Bloomsbury people live in; "The Men"; and then "The Women" of England as he has observed them. In the last, ironically titled, essay, "The Nucleus of a Great Civilisation", he sums up his impressions of the people and the city he has been experiencing over a ten-week period.

James resigned from the position of Lecturer in English Literature and History at the Government Training College in Trinidad to go to England. It is probable that he was the one unnamed passenger on the *M.S. Magdalena*, which left Trinidad for Barbados on Saturday 27 February, 1932 (see Editorial Note, p. xxx). He stayed in Bridgetown for a week, enjoyed tours to different parts of the island arranged by his hosts, and delivered a lecture on "Crown Colony Government in Trinidad" at the Forum Club on Wednesday 2 March. The date of his arrival in Barbados, and other details about his visit, are given in the article on "Barbados and Barbadians".

This article must have been sent from Barbados, since the first instalment was published two days after he arrived in England. Towards the end of the first instalment, James makes a remark that conveys his temper at the time and suggests the need he must have been feeling for space and distance: "It is a pleasant thing to be no longer that model of all propriety, a teacher, and that model of subservience, a Government servant." He was also leaving behind the person he had married in 1926, a young woman of half-Chinese, half-African descent. He told his second wife Constance Webb, to whom he wrote intense letters for eight years before she agreed to marry him, that he wrote to Juanita every Friday for three years before he married her. (See *Special Delivery: The Letters of C.L.R. James to Constance Webb 1939–1948*, 1996.)

James travelled third class out of Barbados on the *M.S. Colombia,* arriving in Plymouth, England, on Friday 18 March. He must have had letters of introduction and contacts, for his "Tribute to Lord Harris" appeared in the *Times* of London on 29 March. Although he seems to have been afflicted with something that made it difficult for him to write, James was prolific. He produced quickly, and it looks as if the post wasn't too bad: his "Visit to the Science and Art Museums" was published in the *Port of Spain Gazette* on 22 May. Between 21 June and 28 August, the *Gazette* published six pieces in a series called "London: First Impressions". These six essays and the earlier account of his visits to the museums form the present volume, *Letters from London.*

The concerns in *Letters from London* are very different to the concerns in those West Indian works of the 1950s and 1960s that are referred to as the literature of exile. It is worth reminding ourselves. After the Second World War, West Indians by the thousands took advantage of their passport status as "citizens of the United Kingdom and Colonies" to carry out what the Jamaican poet Louise Bennett described in a famous poem as colonisation in reverse. By 1956, the annual figure was over twenty-five thousand migrants, and in the early 1960s, as Independence approached and Britain began making moves to shut the door by means of the Commonwealth Immigration Bill, the figure climbed to over fifty thousand per year.

The migrations of the 1950s and early 1960s included ordinary citizens seeking economic opportunity, and driven writers anxious to practise and live off their craft or calling. Of the books that record this movement of people, its social, economic and psychological traumas, and the discoveries it brought, Sam Selvon's *The Lonely Londoners* (1956) and George Lamming's *The Pleasures of Exile* (1960), or at least their titles, have become emblematic.

No West Indian going to England before or after the 1950s would have been able to ignore the existence of race and colour prejudice. James declares in this volume's fifth essay, "The Men", that "the average man in London is eaten up with colour prejudice"; he warns "Mr. Black Man" that in England he should watch his step because of the colour bugbear; and, asserting that this is a big subject, he promises: "I am going to tackle it someday in the way it deserves."

For all that, James's essays of 1932 are in the nature of a report on the experiences of an individual who does not tell us he is feeling cold, who does not talk about his money problems, who does not dwell on race or colour, and who does not raise with us any questions about place or placelessness. And if his account differs from the accounts relating to the mass migration, it is also unlike the response of an earlier individual emigrant.

For the literary historian, the most famous of the individual emigrants to England before James was a white West Indian teenager from Dominica called Jean Rhys. Rhys's experience of England and the English before the First World War, emphatically a young woman's experience, is contained in her brilliant novel *Voyage in the Dark*, which was published only in 1934. There is no sign that James read any of Rhys's books during his first sojourn in England between 1932 and 1938. He would certainly have been responsive, however, to Rhys's sketches of young women adrift in the city with the will but not the economic means or the intellectual equipment to sustain individual freedom. Although his observations about English repression and coldness are not as extensive as hers, and although he does not go so far as to celebrate negritude, there is enough in the essays to suggest that his attitude was consistent with hers. But these similarities only serve to emphasise a fundamental difference in their approaches to England. Hers was a voyage in the dark. His was a pilgrimage to a place of light and learning.

In *Beyond a Boundary* James recalls the conquering hero boarding the boat for the Mother Country: "I was about to enter the arena where I was to play the role for which I had prepared myself. The British intellectual was going to Britain." In *Letters from London* we can indeed see James doing some of the things he had been primed to do by his formal education at Q.R.C. and by the influence of his masters. Especially influential was the school's beloved principal William Burslem, a Cambridge graduate, whom James describes as an Englishman of the nineteenth century, "part Pickwick, part Dr. Johnson, part Samuel Smiles".

In England, James visits art galleries, museums, bookshops; takes in concerts and plays; attends lectures; he reads plays and poems together with friends; peruses fresh copies of the *Times*, the *Daily Herald,* the *New Statesman and Nation* and the *Times Literary Supplement* in bed on a Friday morning; and he takes part in talk sessions going on through the night into the early hours of the morning. In "The Bloomsbury Atmosphere" he shows familiarity with the canonical figures of English literature, is fully conversant with the latest literary trends as well as the gossip, enjoys the bombs (allusive or direct) thrown at other writers by Edith Sitwell, and is pleased to be the brightest boy in the class, identifying William Faulkner as the young American writer whose name she refuses to give, and surprising her by picking up a reference to the musician Constant Lambert. He puts an impressing question to Miss Sitwell, and after her lecture he is pleased to be invited to come up to the platform and speak to her.

The lecturer evades James's question about technique in modern poetry with a theory that "no woman could ever write a really great sonnet . . . technique is largely a matter of physique . . . [no] woman is strong enough physically to weight the syllables as a man can in order to strengthen the lines." James seems to take this nonsense seriously, and doesn't press for a response to his argument that a poet is foremost "a man of strong feeling and delicate nerves" and is interested in technique only as a means of finding the best way to express what is in him. James's observation that it is untalented people with no poetic feelings and nothing to say who most fiddle with technique is still true. I suspect that he might want to extend the remark to those who fiddle with theory today.

The British intellectual may have been playing himself, but the theorist of comprehensive social and human transformation was stirring in the depths. The question James put to the English writer in 1932 is part of a lifelong interest in a number of questions that were clearly, for him, questions about Art: the connection between form and feeling; the relationship between the individual and society; and the tensions between the needs of the personal life and the demands of the movement or group. James's later articulations of the case become infinitely more complex than the commonsense formulation in the early essay. We can appreciate the complexity of the process of social formation, and we can begin to gauge the subterranean and submarine connections between the person and the movement, art and society, poetry and revolution, in James's letters to Constance Webb, especially the cluster written in July 1944. But James is already heading in that direction in the essay of 1932.

While James the British intellectual is immersing himself in the student life of the place, he is looking around him. James does not attempt to imbue the landlady and the lodging house and the English house with the symbolic and culturally hostile qualities that Rhys the novelist suggests so brilliantly in *Voyage in the Dark*. He nevertheless devotes a whole essay to houses. He is impressed by the private houses in the suburbs which are beautifully wallpapered, comfortably furnished, graced with piano, equipped with bookcase, however rubbishy the books, and decorated here and there with a painting or watercolour or etching. He makes a comparison with Trinidad: "Here, in general arrangement and regard for comfort and appearance combined, they have our people of a corresponding class beaten to bits." Nevertheless, he does not like "fidgeting about with teacups and bits of cake", and he prefers the company of Bloomsbury people. He spends more time describing the places where the students, visitors and unmarried middle-class people berth.

The average lodging house is not so much a house as a set of rooms in one big house stretching from one end of the street to the other. A narrow staircase leads to a cramped landing on each floor. Each room has one door and one window that looks out either to walls, the tops of buildings, and the neighbour's cramped backyard, or, if you have a front room, to the windows and walls, windows and walls, of the long building exactly like yours on the other side of the street. On the ground floor, towards the back, are "the lavatory and the unfrequented bathroom." Your room may have a few good chairs, even a good bed, and you may replace some of the furnishings. "But whatever you do, the loneliness of the room is dreadful. When you lock the door you are in a world of your own. . . . You see no one, you hear no one. . . . Who are living in the same house with you, you do not know."

In "Triumph", his short story of 1929, James presents vivid characters and bold actions, uses mock-heroic language and realistic description, to give a stark picture of the urban "yard" which housed the assortment of people migrating to the capital city Port of Spain, from other parts of Trinidad and other islands. The yard is a dynamic community. The depressing surroundings cannot quench the appetite for life or slow the energy of the yard-dwellers. There is infighting among the women, but it is they who hold the side together.

James makes not a single reference to the life of the Port of Spain yard in "The Houses", but he breaks into Trinidad English to comment on these blocks of cells that amazingly began their lives as dwelling houses for families: "How a man could build such a prison for himself to live in or, having a little money, consent to live in one, is beyond my understanding."

In "The Men", he throws in a number of episodes to illustrate the commonly held belief that Englishmen do not speak to one another unless they have been introduced; the lack of social ease of English people; and the English reluctance to intrude on other people even to offer help, for fear of being rebuffed. These are not major insights. Neither is his demonstration that the English, whether in England or overseas, have a burdensome respect for rank, class and prestigious institutions. "More than any creole, white or black, [in Trinidad] they lose their heads at the prospect of contact with the great." The Q.R.C. principal was beside himself with excitement when the school was promised a brief visit by the Governor on his way to somewhere else.

Many of the things James is seeing around him in the England to which he has journeyed make him feel superior. And the men irritate him. He notices that at dances or parties there are few Englishmen, and those who are there sit in corners and glower and look as dissatisfied as possible. He doesn't quite say they are like dogs in a manger. But they get him specially vexed when they show resentment at white girls having anything to do with black men. One night he is sitting in an underground train and two giggling young women, on the platform waiting for another train, exchange appreciative and safe glances with him. As the train moves off he gives them a grave bow and a faint smile, and they laugh more than ever. An Englishman sitting next to him had witnessed the scene: "as the train moved off he glared and glared at the girls and shuffled his feet, and glared at me and looked me up from head to foot, and squirmed and twisted like a man suffering from an acute attack of dysentery or colitis."

Another time, he and a woman friend were returning from an evening out. James reports viciously: "In the lift with us was an Englishman, an ordinary, middle-class, commonplace Englishman. There are millions like him all around you in London every day, the kind of person I would not walk five yards out of my way to meet, except for the sake of curiosity and to find out what was in his *Daily Express,* cinema-fed mind. But he, this Anglo-Saxon member of a ruling race, despised me to such an extent that he could not contain his wrath at seeing me with a girl who was not from the street."

James returns to the question of colour and the attitudes of English men in the essay on "The Women". He has known English girls as pure friends, nothing more, and he has found English women considerate towards foreigners. But it is the men who force them to act as if they have colour prejudice. The problem is that "the English native is so dull and glum and generally boorish in his manners, that the girls turn with relief from these dreadful Englishmen to the smiling and good-natured West Indians. At which the Englishman sits in a corner and scowls and makes himself as unpleasant as possible."

Of James's observations in these essays, the most worthwhile arise from his strong personal interest in women and his growing awareness of the habit of cinema-going among ordinary people, especially women.

Women of an intellectual bent or women with whom he can have nightlong conversations are his constant companions in the two Bloomsbury essays, and he very often prefers them to their boyfriends or husbands. In "The Women" he attempts to be analytical, dividing women into different groups. He has not seen much of "the really delicately bred upper-middle-class type", nor presumably was he familiar with any of "the graceful women you catch glimpses of on a morning stepping from the pavement to the Rolls-Royce or Daimler, nothing superfluous, all cut and line".

But he cites the girl to whom he had been directed by a friend in Trinidad as a good introduction to the women of England, because of her independence, her ease, and her total lack of constraint. Whatever their class, the women seem to have got rid for the most part of male complexes. The Bloomsbury or student type, with as much education as a man, may be inclined to be careless about her clothes, but she is good company and wants men to treat her as an individual, making no concessions to her as a woman. She carries this to the length of paying her share and not having doors opened for her. To James, these are wonderful companions—quick, full of humour and brimming with ideas, willing to argue fiercely, but preserving "a certain grace and delicacy which is peculiar to women." But these are not the "normal type", they are not "the average working girl, working in a bookshop, draper's shop, bureau of some sort, the million and one occupations which London offers."

The normal type in James's classification lives on her own, has a meagre wage, husbands her resources cleverly and with imagination, and is prepared to scramble and jostle because young men do not give way to her on crowded streets, buses, or anywhere. These are the girls of more or less slender means described in the latter part of "The Houses", girls who live in those imprisoning Bloomsbury rooms and have to get out and find someone to go out with. James links them with the large numbers of better-off married women with time on their hands: "They are the most interesting phenomena of the place to me, these women. They fill the cinemas from twelve in the day to twelve at night seeking vicariously or intensifying their restless craving for excitement. They are modern. They are urban— a bad combination. Emancipated. They have their liberty but they don't know what to do with it."

James's sociology may be amateurish, but in these essays he has picked up on the failure of society to adjust to the growing liberation of women in a world becoming more and more fragmented. He has also noticed, without knowing that he has noticed it, the emerging of a new art form responsive to the needs of masses of people. Five years after his arrival in America, in a letter to Constance Webb, James writes as if he has begun to understand what he had picked up in his image of women filling the cinemas: "The movies, even the most absurd Hollywood movies, are an expression of life, and being made for people who pay their money, they express what people need— that is what they miss in their own lives. . . . Like all art, but more than most, the movies are not only a reflection, but an extension of the actual . . . an extension of the actual along the lines which people feel are lacking and possible in the actual."

Maisie in James's novel *Minty Alley* abandons Haynes, who is a dead loss as a man, and sets out for America seeking fulfilment. But it is in his letters to

Constance Webb, his encouraging of Constance to fulfil her possibilities, to follow the powerful impulse "from inside" to be an artist, it is in these letters that James develops the complex question of the plight of modern woman and the remaking of modern society that forces itself upon him in the essays of 1932. The plain fact is that, in 1932 in England, James saw women refusing domesticity without choice, and coming to the city to seek another life, only to find that they were still a long way from having rooms of their own.

It did not take James long to realise that the England he loved and subscribed to was the England of Hobbes and other great writers, the England out of which had come the cricket ethic and the English public school code associated with Thomas Arnold, famous headmaster of Rugby school.

The England he has landed in is another country. It does not impress him. He is not impressed by the traffic. He is not impressed by the buildings. The fine paintings in the galleries are not paintings by British artists. The music at the concerts is not the music of English composers. He is not impressed by the current crop of politicians. He cannot find achievement in any sphere today. He cannot find the particular quality of the English people. Most of "The Nucleus of a Great Civilisation" is a great putdown of the English.

If James could be so critical of the England he was now visiting, it was partly because he was measuring it against standards derived from his sound colonial education, and partly because the alternative education he had absorbed in Trinidad was making him see the world differently to how his formal education had been attempting to arrange it.

James tells us rather extravagantly in *Beyond a Boundary* that long before he was ten years old he was a British intellectual, an alien in his own environment and among his own people. It is necessary to describe James's alternative education at this point. If we reverse the emphasis of his statement in chapter three of *Beyond a Boundary,* we can say that his alternative education began early and not by his will: "I would not deny that early influences I could know nothing about had cast me in a certain mould or even that I was born with certain characteristics." What we can now register is that while reading English literature and watching from the famous window as the characters of native cricket made their commanding entrances and unmarked exits, the child was selecting, and fastening on to, the things that could make him whole, and he was concocting his own version of the British intellectual.

It was a mutation that brought distress to those who expected him to bow uncritically to the formal process at Q.R.C. and the values it served. The little boy did not live up to his scholastic potential. Doing things his own way, he mastered, nevertheless, the principles of cricket and English literature. It is difficult to measure and identify the nebulous ways in which James was taking possession of the imported items even as they were possessing him, but the results are plain enough in his essays, lectures and commentaries.

James's account of what was happening to him in the fourteen years he spent in Trinidad between leaving Q.R.C. and setting out for England can be misleading. He was playing cricket, writing about cricket, reading about cricket and making scrapbooks; teaching, writing and taking part in the activities of literary and cultural groups; and reading the major English literary journals and discussing the great writers, ancient and modern. James says that in this period he was living abroad intellectually and what he was doing involved him with the people around him only in the most abstract way. "In politics I took little interest. I taught in schools but there were no controversies on education."

But after this emphatic declaration, James goes on in *Beyond a Boundary* to describe how all this changed towards the end of the fourteen years, and his experiences at the time allow us to see the process by which he was coming into full realisation of the complexities of race and colour that the artificial hemisphere of school might have tried to exclude. In his last year at Q.R.C. he tried to enlist in the Merchants' Contingent to go to England in the last year of the First World War. He was rejected on sight. After Q.R.C., he agonised over whether he should join Shannon, the cricket club of the black lower-middle class, or Maple, which had been founded on the principle of racial exclusiveness, but which was willing to accept him. The young colonial joined Maple.

Soon he was writing, and encouraging others to write, Trinidadian literature. He joint-edited the two issues of the magazine *Trinidad*. He published five short stories, including the seminal "yard" story "Triumph", and "Turner's Prosperity", a sharp look at self-defeating lower-middle-class opportunism and greed. He crossed swords with a British scientist on the pseudo-science projected by racists, in "The Intelligence of the Negro". He wrote a brilliant portrait of the mulatto lawyer Michel Maxwell Philip, author of the first Trinidadian novel, *Emmanuel*

Appadocca (1854), celebrating Philip's courageous struggle against social and cultural pressures and the racial discrimination that held back his career.

In *Beyond a Boundary* James describes at last how his conversations with Learie Constantine made him see the politics in all his activities, including cricket. "My sentiments were in the right place but I was still enclosed within the mould of nineteenth century intellectualism. Unknown to me, however, the shell had been cracked. Constantine's conversations were always pecking at it." And he describes how the labour disturbances in the island and the activities of the labour leader Captain A.A. Cipriani drove him into a study of the history and the political development of his island. "By the end of the twenties the political situation in the island was developing rapidly. Captain Cipriani, a local white man, was an elected member of the Legislative Council. In that body, the Governor had a firm official majority, able to keep the elected members quiet even if they sought to do anything more than talk. Cipriani, however, built a mass labour movement and as this grew so did his power in the Legislature. This was *real.* "

When James left Trinidad in 1932 he was carrying material for his *Life of Captain Cipriani: An Account of British Government in the West Indies,* and the notes on West Indian cricket that would allow him to work with Constantine on the black cricketer's life. "The British intellectual was going to Britain", James announced, but the manuscripts in his hands were the product of his alternative education.

It is James's alternative education that provides the punch in *Letters from London.* After enthusing about Bloomsbury life and the Bloomsbury atmosphere

James pulls back to deliver home truths to his readers: "And now I have something to say, something which seems to run counter to the spirit of all that I have written. Let no one who wishes to write believe that all I have described is life. In one important sense it is not life at all. It is a highly artificial form of living and I would not be surprised if a great deal of what modern work suffers from is not to be traced to that very cause." James could write this because he had experienced and written about the life of the "yard" in his island, and because he was at the centre of a literary movement determined to marry short story and calypso traditions and to bring the marginalised people and the too-long neglected ideas and feelings of the West Indian masses into fiction.

In "The Nucleus of a Great Civilisation" he looks hard for what is distinct or distinctly English about the English, and for a long time comes up with nothing. In his mind are the vivid people of the West Indies he has been discovering—in his writing, in his growing understanding of cricket as Constantine lived it and played it, and among the revolutionary men and women of the labour movements of the 1920s in Trinidad.

Of the movement of the people inspired by Cipriani's leadership, James had written with emphasis, "this is *real*." And now, hearing how the whole town of Nelson had gone on strike and brought down the cinema owners who were messing with the conditions in which the newest of the popular arts was being delivered to the people, James makes the connection. This is real too.

The nucleus of a great civilisation was not London. It was ordinary people like the people of his island. Like the people of Nelson where Constantine lived, and where James was about to go and get into the real. "I could forgive England all the vulgarity and all the depressing disappointment of London for the magnificent spirit of these north country working people."

Editorial Note

In 1931 C.L.R. James, already a prominent intellectual figure in his home island, decided to leave Trinidad early the following year for England, with the encouragement of his friend Learie Constantine. His plan was "to write books", as he says in *Beyond a Boundary*.

The exact dates of his departure and arrival were long forgotten. Thirty years later, James wrote that "in March 1932 I boarded the boat for Plymouth." A bit of historical arithmetic suggests that he actually left on 27 February. Thanks to an article called "Barbados and Barbadians" (giving a detailed itinerary of his visit) published in March 1932 in the *Port of Spain Gazette,* we know that, after leaving Trinidad, James spent a week in Barbados, from Sunday 28 February to either Sunday 5 or Monday 6 March. The only boat that left Port of Spain harbour in time to arrive at Bridgetown on the morning of 28 February was the *M.S. Magdalena* of the Hamburg-Amerika line, which sailed on Saturday 27. The *Port of Spain Gazette* listed the passengers on board the *Magdalena* that day; James is not among them. But, intriguingly, the *Gazette* also reported that fourteen passengers were on board. Only thirteen are listed by name. The evidence suggests that James was the unnamed fourteenth passenger on the *Magdalena*.

After his week in Barbados, James boarded the *M.S. Colombia* of the Royal Netherlands Steamship Company. Making good time, the *Colombia* put in at the port of Plymouth on Friday 18 March, 1932, and British immigration records confirm that James entered the United Kingdom on this date.

The plan was that he would join Constantine and his family at their house in Nelson, Lancashire, but first James spent a couple of months in London, investigating the possibilities of the empire's capital. It is not known exactly how long he was in London, but it seems he stayed there at least ten weeks, and probably left for Nelson in late May. His initial observations of the metropolis are recorded in the essays collected in this volume.

These seven essays were originally published in the *Port of Spain Gazette* in 1932. The first of them was reprinted in Anna Grimshaw's *C.L.R. James Reader* in 1992, with the title "Bloomsbury: An Encounter with Edith Sitwell". The others have not been in print for seventy years.

Six of these essays originally appeared as a series under the title "London: First Impressions". The first two were published on 21 and 22 June, 1932, numbered "1" and "2" but without subtitles. After a gap of more than a month the third appeared on 27 July with the subtitle "The Houses" and numbered "2" in erroneous repetition. The rest of the series continues the numbered sequence from this: "No. 3: The Men" (4 August), "No. 4: Women" (11 August) and "No. 5: The Nucleus of a Great Civilisation" (28 August).

I have preserved the original subtitles, supplying a definite article in one instance. Instead of "An Encounter with Edith Sitwell" I have preferred to title the first essay "The Bloomsbury Atmosphere", since this is what James actually sets out to describe therein. Inasmuch as the second essay takes up directly where the first leaves off, I have called it "Bloomsbury Again".

The first essay in this volume is not part of the "London: First Impressions" series and in fact appeared a month earlier, on 22 May. Its original title was "A Visit to Science and Art Museums". Again I have taken the liberty of supplying a definite article.

The text of all seven essays was transcribed from hard copies of the microfilmed *Gazette*. A few corrections were required to obvious typographical mistakes. The spelling of a few words has been modernised. It is impossible to know to what degree James's original text was modified by *Gazette* editors or sub-editors. No manuscript appears to have survived; and in fact James mentions that at least some of the essays were dictated rather than written, which accounts for the occasional conversational looseness of the syntax. I have felt free, therefore, to make minor amendments, such as removing an unnecessary "that" or two, in the interest of the prose; or inserting paragraph breaks into a run-on passage of dialogue for easier reading. My chief principle, however, has been to preserve James's distinctive narrative voice.

Some of the essays originally appeared with crossheads (minor subheads dividing the text into sections) inserted by *Gazette* sub-editors. These I have removed.

Several of James's literary references were slightly misquoted, suggesting his reliance on memory. I have corrected these in the text but recorded the errors in the notes, in case these should be of interest.

Finally, despite the absence of actual correspondence, the title *Letters from London* seems appropriate to this collection because of the essays' immediacy and informality and because of the strong impression they give of the author's personality. Many of his original readers in Trinidad were friends and colleagues who no doubt would have followed James's reports as eagerly as if they were personal epistles. Contemporary readers, I hope, will also feel a sense of intimacy, sharing these impressions and what they reveal of the hopes, wishes and worries of the thirty-one-year-old C.L.R. James.

A section of notes located unobtrusively after the final essay will, I hope, illuminate some of the less familiar persons and events mentioned by James.

I wish to thank Paul Bary of the Latin American Library of Tulane University and Richard Phillips of the Latin American Collection at the George A. Smathers Libraries of the University of Florida, for providing me with hard copies from their microfilm holdings of the *Port of Spain Gazette*. Such hard copies proved impossible to obtain from any library in Trinidad. The reader will excuse my remarking that this is most unfortunate.

Ken Ramchand, in addition to writing the introduction preceding this note, gave valuable advice on all aspects of editing this book.

Damien Smith visited the Public Record Office at Kew to examine the British immigration records for 1932 and establish the exact date of James's arrival in the United Kingdom.

Jim Murray, Director of the C.L.R. James Institute in New York, gave both advice and vigorous encouragement.

Much of the research for this volume was done online; nowadays anyone with an Internet connection has the approximate equivalent of a decent re-

search library at his round-the-clock disposal. I feel
~~obliged, therefore, to thank also the proprietors of~~
Google and xrefer.

Nicholas Laughlin
Diego Martin, Trinidad and Tobago

A Visit to the Science and Art Museums

(Originally published in
the *Port of Spain Gazette*,
22 May, 1932)

I hadn't intended to spend much time there. I was on my way to the Victoria and Albert Museum. But one of the men I was with, John Ince, is clever at engines and, at least to an ignoramus like myself, learned in the mysteries of mechanics. He persuaded me to go in and, I do not know why, the place had a surprising effect on me. "Why haven't we got such a place at home; or at least something like it?"

It is the Science Museum and as soon as you go in you are knocked silly by the sight of the airplane in which Lieutenant Stanforth won the Schneider Trophy at a speed of 407 miles an hour; that is to say, from Port of Spain to St. Joseph in one minute, quicker than the thoughts of many estimable people of my acquaintance.

The plane is the most beautiful thing in the museum and one of the most beautiful things I have seen in London. It is like one of the graceful women you catch glimpses of on a morning stepping from the pavement to the Rolls-Royce or the Daimler, nothing superfluous, all cut and line; and it looks so light, you feel that for a bet you could go below it, steady it on your right hand, and walk around with it just as you give a ride to a tiny child of which you are fond. Technical description is beyond me (despite much exposition by Ince) but the body is like nothing so much as a long fish and the stays (I hope this is the correct word) look as if they would break if the machine went at seven miles an hour, far less 407. They are about half an inch by an eighth. In fact the whole thing looks like a toy, and it is a thing for photographers to think about, that what has been built solely for utility turns out to be so beautiful. I often used to wonder formerly what was the use of spending so much time and effort on mere speed. Two hundred miles an hour, three hundred miles an hour, four hundred miles an hour—who cares? And among the useful pieces of information printed near the exhibit is an answer to my question, which I had always secretly thought represented rather a reactionary point of view. To get more speed means such research and effort in design, engines, material, etc., that scientific knowledge goes forward. I am satisfied. May they do a thousand miles before I die!

After such a beginning the rest was bound to be pleasing. There was the first power-driven airplane (1903), the machine of the Wright Brothers. In some of the older relics there are dummy figures showing where the pilot stood or sat or lay, and these Wrights were certainly men of genius. To me it seems that they built their plane and clean forgot, as is the way of men absorbed in their work, that they might as well think of themselves a little. In that 1903 plane there was no place for the pilot. He lay flat on his stomach on the lower wing, which meant, of course, that when the plane did anything else but balance steadily, he had not only to keep her steady, but see about himself too. Maybe he was tied down. It is only when you look at the thing that you realise not only the mechanical ingenuity but the enormous physical courage of the men who would trust their lives in such a position to such a rickety contrivance. Rickety, because while the Schneider plane is a thing of wonder and looks as if it flew straight from the inventor's brain, the Wright plane looks like wire and canvas. Given the design, two or three good carpenters could probably turn it out in a few days. And yet the Wright plane is by far the greater performance of the two. Without it the others had not been.

Then, along the wall, the development of the airplane from 1903 to 1928, small models of every type, 1906, 1908, many between 1914 and 1918, up to 1928. On the other side, the development of the balloon and airship from 1783 to 1919, models again. Amy Johnson's plane. Nothing to look at though. . . .

Then gliders, not models but originals, and some very curious indeed. One Frost, for instance, in 1902 modelled the wings of his glider (or maybe he would have called it a plane) on the wings of a bird. He succeeded admirably, and the two wings of the invention look exactly like the wings of some great eagle. Alas, in the notice below I read, "There is no record of the machine having successfully raised itself in the air." I am smiling but there is a tragedy here. For twenty years work had gone into the design and construction of these wings. Life can be hard.

I do not intend to make a detailed inventory of all I saw. I am not competent to do so. There are models of everything, and in some cases the actual old airship, or car, or steam-engine. One or two exhibits, however, struck me more than the rest. *Miss England* I was there, the boat in which Sir Henry Segrave did ninety-two miles an hour . . . but as a spectacle it was nothing to the Schneider plane.

It is a pity that Ruskin never saw that plane. He has written magnificently (if a little extravagantly) of the bow of a boat, but had he seen *Miss England I* and the plane side by side, I know which he would have written on. The *Miss England I* propeller, by the way, makes eleven thousand complete revolutions in a minute.

There was an old clock from Wells Cathedral which was working before the end of the fourteenth century. In the middle of the last century new works were installed and the clock was removed to the Museum, where it ticks serenely on, striking the quarters and the hours, and keeping much better time than the brand-new watch which I bought two weeks ago and which (so the hopman says but I don't believe him) is going badly because it is "subject to climatic conditions." I had a good look at that old clock. Rather a dull existence tick-ticking away, with a little recurrent excitement every quarter of an hour. But I couldn't help remembering with envy that in a few years I would probably be gone, while the old beast would probably be there in a thousand years, tick-ticking away, living his narrow but peaceable life.

Models, models, models everywhere, including a model of the Bermuda Dock in 1868 and the model of the dock as it is today, which I noted with great approval, for Bermuda is not exactly the West Indies, but these English people don't know that, and a little deception in a good cause need involve no lengthy arguments as to the end justifying the means. Many of these models work by compressed air. Press a button and they start immediately. And of course the children have a glorious time. They walk from case to case pressing buttons, and the fresh faces and the bright eyes glow as the wheels start to spin. I had a press myself; chose a large case with fifteen wheels and things (a model of I know not what, I chose it because it was large)—pressed the button rather gingerly—and, by Jove, everything started to move. I felt like an inventor.

Now, as I said at the start, why couldn't we have some models at home? An attendant told me that some of them (though not many) are made on the premises by the museum staff, while a good many are sent by private firms. We can't afford galleries of beautiful pictures, statues, and works of art (though we could have reproductions and plaster-casts, as in Canada), but we certainly could have a small museum of models of the type which predominate in this science museum. And one reason why this struck me so forcibly is because of a boy I saw there. Most of the other children (and at least one grownup) were sightseeing and pressing buttons for the fun of the thing. But there was this boy, a boy of about fourteen, thin, with a thin, keen, rather handsome face, leaning over *Miss England I*, examining the dials and steering gear. Sir Henry Segrave never looked at them with more concentration. You could almost see the boy's mind growing. So Galileo must have looked at the pendulum, noting how evenly it swung; or Newton at the apple, wondering why it fell. Museums, galleries, etc., are for the general public, it is true. What the general public learns there is a debatable point. But the one-in-a-thousand boy is the justification for all such expenditure. He sees and sees and sees all that has ever been done and then, if he has the right stuff in him, his mind moves forwards maybe only a little way, but still a little way. Henry Ford knows this very well. He is devoting a fortune to making a museum in America where there will be models of everything from the beginning of time, Adam's spade, Noah's ship, etc., etc., down to the latest of everything.

We, in Trinidad, know what the answer to any such effort, if it ever is made, will be. No money, and probably a hint that, "Oh, the people will not be interested," the people this and the people that. But all this talk about the people—I have been to the National Gallery twice. Free lectures are provided daily—a lecturer goes round discoursing on points in the pictures, their history, etc. The first day I went there were about twenty people, the second day not so many. The heart of London, mind you, eight million people, after centuries of civilisation. Let any idle mathematician work out what fraction of a person would represent the Trinidadian corresponding proportionately to the twenty whom I saw representing the eight million. When you move around this place and see the opportunities the people have, the way everything is put in their way, and kept ready for whomever may want it; and then stop and think for a minute of the conditions in the West Indies, Trinidad and poor Barbados, the wonder is not that the creoles do so little but that they do so well. All that any middle-class Englishman needs is a little ambition. If he has that, the way to achievement and success is wide open. Of course, the competition is keen, but there is competition everywhere. The fact remains that a man in this country can make himself a highly cultured person by merely providing himself with a thick pair of boots to walk from place to place. Free. Free. Free. Everything free. Some people say that there has never been a Beethoven player like Arthur Schnabel. You may, if you like, pay twenty-one shillings to hear him, but either the Government or the London County Council provides free concerts and Schnabel has played at one of these. They don't run down the people here. They provide the best and then beg them to come and take advantage of it. And when they don't come they hold meetings and rack their brains to try and encourage them.

But as I said, my aim that morning was not the Science Museum. I went finally to the Victoria and Albert Museum—pictures, books, statues, tapestries, woodwork, everything. I went there, so to speak, on business. I wanted a book. The bookseller could not recommend one of the type I wanted, but he told me to go to the Victoria and Albert Museum where there is a splendid library of books on art—the best in England. There I could see the books they had and decide which one I wanted. Admirable. The librarian showed me thirty catalogues, each eighteen inches long, twelve inches wide and three inches thick. But alphabetical order is alphabetical order, in one volume or fifty. I chose my books, wrote them on a card and was shown to a seat. In two minutes appears a man with the volumes in his hand. In five minutes I decide on the one I want, and the whole thing is over. A wonderful country, this.

So I decide to look around. Room after room. First editions of Shakespeare, Japanese bronzes, sketches by Picasso. I am hungry and have lunch—on the premises. Round and round again. And being hungry again, have tea. And go round again and lose myself—though I meet more attendants than visitors—and, by great good fortune, come down some steps and find myself near to the same door that I went in. So I take that as a hint from Providence and decide that I have had enough for one day and must go home. And then comes the thrill of the day. For, walking out, I cast my eye to the left and see a Rodin statue which I have read about in Orpen's *Outline of Art. John the Baptist* Rodin called it, but it is no more John the Baptist than I am John the Baptist. It is a statue of a naked man walking, that's all, neither more nor less, and Rodin was persuaded to call it *John the*

Baptist. But all that is irrelevant. The only thing that matters is the statue. In the basement of the British Museum are plaster-casts of the *Apollo Belvedere* and the *Venus de Milo*, but on the Day of Judgement, the twentieth century will be able to look the old Greeks in the eye and say, "We admit that yours are the best, but . . ." and then produce the Rodin. No one who sees it can pass it by. That is one thing with the plastic arts. You need some training in literature, and more in music, but any fool who will take the trouble to look can see a picture or a statue. I was dreadfully tired out but the thing made me fresh again.

Ours is not the only age of scientific enterprise and multitudinous organisation.

In one year they sent a million fighters forth
    South and North,
And they built their gods a brazen pillar high
    As the sky,
Yet reserved a thousand chariots in full force—
    Gold, of course.

Oh heart! oh, blood that freezes, blood that
    burns! . . .

Browning was speaking of a girl, but there are other things than girls that make the blood burn. The Rodin statue is one. I sat and watched it and when the body is still the mind moves. I reflected that a Greek who lived two thousand years ago could have sat with me and watched. He would have seen it with much the same eyes and feelings that I did. But the Schneider plane would have been meaningless to him. Three thousand years from now, some wanderer from the West Indies will walk down Exhibition Road. He will go into the Science Museum and see the latest thought-plane. (That vanished type of conveyance, aircraft, will be represented by models.) Will he see Lieutenant Stanforth's plane? Only as one of a crowd of obsolete designs.

But in the Art Museum he will see the statue of the man walking. It will be to him as it is to me. It cannot grow old. It cannot go out of date. It is timeless, made materially of bronze but actually, as has been said of great literature, the precious life-blood of a master spirit.

That is why though I shall sometimes visit the Museum of Science it will always be on my way to the Museum of Art.

The Bloomsbury Atmosphere

(Originally published in
the *Port of Spain Gazette*,
21 June, 1932)

I have been living in London for ten weeks and will give what can only be called first impressions. I have been living in Bloomsbury, that is to say, the students' and young writers' quarter. It is different from Clapham or Ealing—suburbia, as you can imagine—and is in its way distinctive, so absolutely different from life in the West Indies that it stands out as easily the most striking of my first impressions. In later articles I shall go more into detail about such things as have struck me—houses, food, clothes, men, women, the streets, scores of things. But for the present my chief concern will be with Bloomsbury and the Bloomsbury atmosphere. I shall best describe it by not trying to describe it at all, but by merely setting down faithfully the events of three or four days, just as they happened. If there is a lot of "I" and "I" and "I", it cannot be helped. I can only give my own impressions, and what happened to me. To generalise about so large a district and such numbers of people after only ten weeks would be the limit of rashness.

I shall begin with Wednesday the eighteenth of May. I reached home from the city at about half past three, having twice sat before food and both times been unable to eat.

I knew from long experience that I had a sleepless night before me, and to make matters worse my right hand, which had been going for some time, decided finally to go. I tried to write and found that I could not—nervous strain I expect. I went to bed, got out of bed, went to bed again, knocked about the place a bit, tried to read, failed, in fact did not know what to do with myself. But I was in Bloomsbury, so would always find distraction.

Restlessness was the only reason which made me go to a lecture at the Student Movement House by Miss Edith Sitwell. I had promised to go with a girl whom I have met here, extremely interesting, and the only person I have ever met who, if we are looking down a book or newspaper together, has to wait at the end of the page for me, and not by three or four lines, but sometimes by ten. I had almost intended to telephone to say that I was not going, but the prospect of my own company in a room of a Bloomsbury lodging house, aesthetically speaking one of the worst places in the world, made me decide to summon up some energy and go to hear Miss Sitwell. I went over to my friend's room and met there herself and another girlfriend of hers who had ridden five miles to come to the lecture, and was going to ride five miles afterwards to get home. We walked over to the Student Movement House, which is a club for London students, white and coloured, but with its chief aim giving coloured students in London an opportunity to meet together and fraternise with English students, and with one another. The atmosphere of the place is decidedly intellectual, in intention at least.

Now I had heard a lot about Miss Edith Sitwell before. She is supposed to be eccentric, in appearance and manner at least. She and her two brothers, Osbert and Sacheverell, are a family of wealthy people who have devoted themselves to literature (chiefly poetry) and the arts. They have made quite a name for themselves as poets and critics, and although few modern writers have attracted such a storm of hostile criticism, yet that in itself is perhaps a testimony of a certain amount of virility in their work. Today, however, they have won their position and are among the first flight of the younger generation of English writers. Miss Edith Sitwell, I had been told in Trinidad, rather posed. She wore robes, not dresses, and, to judge from her photographs, was not only handsome but distinctly evil-looking in appearance. She had an underlip that seemed the last word in spite and malice, and in nearly every photograph that I had seen a rebellious lock of hair waved formidably about her forehead.

At a quarter past eight there was the usual whisper and the lady walked into the room. If ever rumour had been lying, this certainly was a case. She did wear robes, some old brocaded stuff, dark in colour with a pattern of some kind. The waist was about six inches below where the waist of the ordinary dress is and the skirt was not joined to the bodice in a straight line but by means of many half circles looking somewhat like the rim of an opened umbrella. Women will know the kind of design I mean. But the chief thing was that she could carry the dress. She is tall and, though mature, still slim, and the dress fit beautifully. But even more remarkable than the dress was the face, a thin, aristocratic, well-formed face, very sharp and very keen. The lip I saw later did look spiteful at times but it was only when she shot an arrow at some of her fellow poets and writers, and, to speak the truth, she had a good many to shoot. The lock of hair I can say nothing about, because she wore a small white cap which would have kept the most rebellious locks in order. She stood on the little platform to address us, a striking figure, decidedly good-looking, and even more decidedly a personality. Perhaps the outstanding impression was one of fitness and keenness together, the same impression I had got from a bronze head of her brother I had seen in the Tate.

I do not intend to go into her lecture, which consisted partly of readings from her own and other works and partly of short dissertations on certain aspects of modern work, the Sitwells being essentially of the modern school. Her voice was not exceptional and she was rather hoarse but she read well. Most interesting to me, however, were the bombs she threw at writer after writer. For a sample, Mr. D.H. Lawrence, who would be judged by most people the finest English writer of the post-war period. Miss Sitwell (sparkling with malicious enjoyment) told us that in the course of a lecture at Liverpool she had defined Mr. Lawrence as the chief of the Jaeger school of poetry. This was reported in the press and a few days afterwards she received a dignified letter from the famous firm of underwear makers, saying that they had noted her remark and would like to know what she meant by that reference to their goods.

Miss Sitwell replied that she had called Mr. Lawrence the head of the Jaeger School because his poetry was like Jaeger underwear, hot, soft and woolly; whereupon the Jaeger Company replied that while their products were soft and woolly they begged to deny that they were in any way hot, owing to their special process which resulted in non-conductivity of heat. Miss Sitwell begged to apologise and asked the Jaeger Company if they could discover a special process for Mr. D.H. Lawrence which would have the same effect of non-conductivity. Unfortunately, Mr. Lawrence died too soon and nothing could be done. That is a sample of the kind of compliment she distributed, and it is only fair to say that she and her two brothers, if they give hard knocks, have received quite as many. Naturally, I was very much interested in all this and soon realised that I had done very well to come. But more was to follow. Speaking of D.H. Lawrence, she said that she did not think much of his work on the whole, that even his novels were very much overrated, and she knew a young American writer of 31 or 32 who was a far finer novelist than D.H. Lawrence. However, wild horses would not drag his name from her.

Of course, that was easy. I told her at once that it was William Faulkner and she rather blinked a bit though honestly I do not think there was much in it. Anyone who is really interested in fiction would at least have heard Faulkner's name.

As the evening progressed Miss Sitwell grew more and more animated, and told us a story of that very brilliant writer who has just died, Mr. Lytton Strachey. To appreciate the story properly, you must understand that Mr. Strachey was a very thin, tall man, well over six feet, with a long beard, and in appearance the essence of calm, assured, dignified superiority. I had heard of this and fortunately had seen, also in the Tate, first, a portrait of Mr. Strachey, full-size, which, though a mediocre painting, gave one some idea of the man, and, secondly, a bust which was an admirable piece of work and gave a strong impression of his personality. To return to Miss Sitwell's story. She said that a young composer, a big bustling fellow, whose name she certainly would not tell us, had met Mr. Strachey at a party. Two years afterwards he met Mr. Strachey at another party, hustled up to him, and said, "Hello! I met you at a party two years ago, didn't I?" Mr. Strachey drew himself up, pointed his beard in the air, and looking serenely over the head of the intruder on his peace said quietly, "Yes, two years ago. A nice long interval, isn't it?" As soon as the meeting was over I went to her and told her that I hoped I wasn't intruding, but I would be glad to know if her young composer was not Constant Lambert. You never saw a woman look so surprised. She had to admit that it was and wanted to know how in the name of heaven I knew that.

I do not know Constant Lambert's music at all, but since the reorganisation of the *New Statesman* as the *New Statesman and Nation* he has been writing music criticism for the new paper, and writes quite well. One day I saw in the *Tatler* or *Sketch* or some picture-book of the kind a photograph of Mr. Constant Lambert and his bride. It was his wife that interested me, however. She was a cute little woman with features rather resembling someone whom I knew, and yet no two women could have looked more different. She was rather a striking little woman in her way, and I looked at the photograph for some time, paying little attention, however, to Mr. Lambert himself, who was big and beefy and burly and looked rather like a prize-fighter. But when Miss Sitwell began her story with this young composer who was so big and who came pushing his way in, then the connection was simple enough. I had one shot and it went straight home.

But before the evening was over, I am afraid I had an argument with the good lady. After the lecture proper came questions when Miss Sitwell sat down and answered whatever anyone chose to ask. Here she was at her best, showed a wide range of reading, was terse and incisive and every now and then, when she got in a particularly good shot which set the house in roars of laughter, her lower lip quivered for a fraction of a second in a fascinating way.

After a while I asked her a question on which I have definite views of my own. There is a lot of experimentation in all modern art today, in technique particularly. People are writing free verse, verse which I believe Shakespeare and Keats and Shelley would find it difficult to recognise as kindred to their own work. Some people say that poetry must find new forms. It is my belief, though only a belief, that a great poet is first and foremost a poet, that is to say, a man of strong feeling and delicate nerves, and secondly a technician and interested in technique, as such only a means of getting the best manner of expressing what he has in him; and I also incline to the belief that if a great poet were born today he could use the traditional forms of verse and write the most magnificent poetry without bothering himself about new forms of poetry and technical experiments and the other preoccupations of most modern writers. These preoccupations it seems to me are things of essentially secondary importance. But with the spread of education and multiplication of books, people with little genuine poetic fire occupy themselves with poetry and thus have to concentrate on technique. Real poetic genius they cannot cultivate, because they have not got it.

At any rate I asked her the question quite straightforwardly.

"Do you believe that a genuine poet coming into the world today would be able to write great poetry in the old traditional form, the sonnet form for instance?" I chose the sonnet particularly. From Sir Thomas Wyatt in the sixteenth century to the present day, Englishmen have written these poems of fourteen lines. Shakespeare and Milton, Keats and Wordsworth, nearly all the great English poets have exercised themselves with the sonnet. Could a modern Shakespeare write a sonnet which would be able to take its place beside the sonnets of Shakespeare or Milton?

Miss S.: To begin with, I do not think that any modern sonnets of the first class have been written since the sonnets of Keats and Wordsworth.

Myself: What about Elizabeth Barrett Browning's *Sonnets from the Portuguese,* particularly the one beginning, "If thou must love me, let it be for nought / Except for love's sake only"?

Miss S.: (shaking her head) No, as a matter of fact I think that no woman could ever write a really great sonnet. I happen to believe that technique is largely a matter of physique. Pope, for instance, though an invalid, had very strong and beautiful hands . . . and I do not think that any woman is strong enough physically to weight the syllables as a man can in order to strengthen the lines.

Myself: But you will admit that the "Ode to a Nightingale" and the "Ode to a Grecian Urn" are magnificent poetry.

Miss E.S.: Yes, certainly.

Myself: But nevertheless Keats was always very frail.

Miss E.S.: Of course I do not mean that to write fine poetry a man must be big and strong like a butcher.

It was the reply of a skilful controversialist. The audience was much amused. And as it was her lecture and not mine I let it pass. Nevertheless I think it was pretty clear to a good many in the hall that she was concerned.

But that is not all there is to it. At odd moments I have been thinking over the matter and while I cannot say that she is right I am becoming less and less able to say that she is wrong. Unfortunately for her I happened to hit almost immediately on the chief example which seems to confound her theories at once. But on close observation even the case of Keats can be defended. Keats's poetry is very beautiful but it is not strong as the work of Shakespeare or Milton is strong; even Shelley, magnificent poet as he is, has force and fire, but not strength in the sense that Shakespeare has strength. Take for instance these two lines from one of the sonnets:

O, how shall summer's honey breath hold out
Against the wrackful siege of battering days.

Against the wrackful siege of battering days. Anyone who reads that aloud can feel the almost physical weight behind the lines. One does not get it often in Keats and in Shelley. And it is particularly the kind of weight that the sonnet form, compact as it is, needs in order that every line of the fourteen should tell. It is not an easy question, and this is not the place to discuss it. Anyway, after many more questions the regular meeting ended. Then came general conversation in which those who wished went up to the platform and talked to Miss Sitwell while the audience broke up into groups. Students went up and came down, but stranger as I was, I did not go, and was talking to a girl who spoke thirteen languages when the chairman touched me on the shoulder. Would I give my name and address to Miss S., and would I come up on the platform and speak to her? Certainly, no one more pleased than I.

Up on the platform Miss Sitwell sat in the centre of a group of students. There was the chairman also and there was a Miss Trevelyan, some relation, I believe, of the Oxford historian. The talk ran chiefly on the work of the moderns. There is no need to go into what was said, except that Miss Sitwell agreed thoroughly with what

I have always felt, that, for instance, to take an outstanding figure among the moderns, while one listens with the greatest interest to the music of Stravinsky, neither he nor any other modern can ever move your feelings as can Bach or Haydn, Mozart or Beethoven. It is the great weakness of most modern work. Well, it ended as all good things have to end. Miss Sitwell promised to send me a book written by her brother in traditional verse. I was bold enough to say that I hoped I would see her again. She said, yes, certainly.

We may seem to have got some distance from Bloomsbury. We have not. That is Bloomsbury. Some group or society is always having lectures or talks by some distinguished person who comes and talks and is always willing to do anything for anyone who wishes assistance or guidance of some sort. On the Sunday following Miss Sitwell's lecture, Mr. Sidney Dark was to speak. Still later in the term Mr. Walter de la Mare is to speak on Modern Fiction. Something of that kind in music, art, literature, architecture, philosophy, history, by the most distinguished persons, day after day. You have your choice. And however distinguished the lecturers, they are always willing to do their very best for anyone who seems more than usually interested.

I went to two lectures by Professor Bidez of the University of Ghent on Greece and the Near East. The lectures were in French and I found them rather difficult to follow, but the man was so interesting that I wrote him a short note asking if there were any small books on the subject, or magazine articles which he himself had written. He did not reply at once, but did so when he reached back home. He wrote that he was delighted to have heard from me, that the interest I took in his subject gave him great pleasure, that my writing him about it meant far more to him than anything which he could do for me. He sent me one of his own articles, signed, as a souvenir, and told me that although he had not written as yet, his book on the subject would soon be published and he would be extremely glad to send me a copy. He does not know me and in all probability never will.

There is the case of John Clarke, who along with law has been doing literature, and economics, and sociology, and goodness knows what not. He attended a series of lectures on sociology given by Mrs. Beatrice Webb, Lord

Passfield's wife. He was not too certain of himself and wrote to her asking for some guidance. He told me that he was surprised at the result. She did not send him information on what books to read, but sent him actual manuscripts, sheets and sheets of her own work. She invited him to tea, filled him with food and knowledge, and told him to come again. That is not exactly Bloomsbury, but it is the atmosphere of Bloomsbury. Anyone who lives in this place for any length of time and remains dull need not worry himself. Nothing he will ever do will help him. He was born that way.

Bloomsbury Again

(Originally published in
the *Port of Spain Gazette*,
22 June, 1932)

We must have left the Student Movement House at about half past eleven. The three of us who had gone went back to where we had come from. We talked for about an hour. Another girl who lives in the same house came in, found that we had been listening to Edith Sitwell, and went upstairs and brought down a small volume of her poetry, which she lent to me. Then the girl who had ridden in set off on her five-mile ride home to Chelsea, the artists' quarter, for she herself is an artist, miniature painting and photography. I was not sleepy, only too wide awake in fact; my friend was not too sleepy either. She is very fond of Tagore. We fiddled about with a volume of Tagore for a few minutes and then started to talk sitting on the floor before the fire. We talked and talked. Suddenly I looked through the window. Outside was unreasonably bright. After another look we realised that it was morning, somewhere near six o'clock. So I had a cup of Oxo and went home to bed. At half past eight I was lying in bed, drowsy but not by any means sleepy, when in comes another friend of mine, a poet and writer of short stories for children, a highly cultivated and charming person. He had heard that I had gone to the lecture. He picked up the volume of Edith Sitwell which I had brought home with me and began to read long extracts. He has a magnificent baritone voice and as a matter of fact has not only lectured in America but has done much speaking over the radio. He read for me about half an hour while I lay covered up in bed and listened. And he was a far better reader than Miss Sitwell was. In fact he has told me that quite a few well known modern poets have asked him to read their verse on platforms instead of reading themselves. When he was tired I got up to dress. He wandered round the room and, seeing a catalogue of gramophone records, began looking it through. We started to talk about music. In his early days before his voice broke he had been a singer of old English songs, ballads and other such songs as suited his voice. The name Handel caught his eye in the catalogue and he suddenly threw it down and began to sing a famous Handel aria, "Where'er you walk." He sang it right through from beginning to end, cadenzas and everything, and it was a grand performance. I stood with one half of my face shaved and the other covered with soap listening to him while, with his hands joined as if on the stage, he gave a concert performance.

At about half past ten he went away and I went out to see after my affairs. When you have had twenty-four hours of almost unceasing excitement without sleep of any kind nature insists that you be quiet. The machinery runs down. So I walked about London very peaceably and got my mind clear on a few knotty points. I did what I had to do and at about half past two walking up Oxford Street I saw Bumpus's, the famous bookshop. There was an exhibition on there free of charge, the library and papers of John Locke, the famous English philosopher. So I went in and had a look. There were the books that the sage used, his desk, his manuscripts, his private notebooks that he kept year after year, making notes of everything that he saw and heard. One of the notebooks was open and I read a note to the effect that a man told him how at a certain place in France five miles from such and such a spot was "a spring which was cold in summer and hot in winter." "This," added Locke, in a touch which I appreciated, "he told me he knew from his own observation." There was the manuscript of the *Essay Concerning Human Understanding*.

There was also one letter in which he wrote to the king begging that his salary of five hundred pounds a year now overdue should be paid to him, for philosophers like other people have to live. I spent about an hour there and saw also some cartoons of famous public men by Powys Evans. I was just in time because the attendant told me that the cartoons were going to be sent off almost at once.

I could not do a stroke of work. Writing was out of the question and I could not even read because I could not make notes. I had intended to go to a lecture on a most intriguing subject: "The Absurdity of Any Mind-Body Relation." But this was to begin at half past and when I reached home at five o'clock I was too tired and lay on the sofa for an hour or so. I had dinner and then went to keep another appointment in the room of a young West African, twenty-one years old, who reads a volume of Proust at a sitting and reads Descartes, Berkeley and Spinoza "in order to train his mind." He and I and the same girl with whom I had talked till six o'clock in the morning had arranged to meet at about eight o'clock. But I went early, and fortunately, because he had gone to the lecture on the Mind-

Body Relation, and he told me all about it before she came. When she did come, after a little talk, we got down to business at once and read Chekov's *Three Sisters*. Home that night at twelve.

I slept a little and next morning being Friday amused myself in bed with the *Times,* the *Daily Herald,* the *New Statesman and Nation,* the *Times Literary Supplement* (which had come in on the Thursday but which I had not read) and the delightful Miss Rebecca West in the *Daily Telegraph* as usual every Friday. In Trinidad you get them all in a bunch two weeks at a time. In London you get them as they come and take them in your stride. This carried me on to about half past one when I went to the Middle Temple seeking some information. There I met Mitra Sinanan and John Clarke. We argued in the Common Room until the caretaker said I had no right there. We argued in the grounds of the Temple, we argued in the Strand, we went into a café and argued again until a waitress came and looked at us so severely that we went outside, went back to the Middle Temple, still arguing, upon which it was nearly six o'clock and as I had a lecture at half past seven I had to run away, being thoroughly tired and hoarse from having talked too much. I delivered the lecture that night to the Society for International Studies. In the very same building Mr. C.F. Andrews was speaking to another society interested in Indian Nationalism and people from his meeting kept on coming into mine. The lecture was fairly successful because after it was finished I received two invitations—one to join the Friends of India Society, which meets on the first Monday of every month, and the other to lecture on any subject connected with the West Indies at the Indian Students' Central Association. You might think that was enough for one day. You simply do not know Bloomsbury.

We reached the Russell Square tube café at about half past eleven to twelve and went in to eat and drink and talk. The president of the society was with us and whispered to me not to take more than a cup of coffee or so because someone had invited him to supper and I could come along. Also if I wished I could bring along an Indian whom I had been talking to along the road. I had met him at a party and liked him because of his genuine reactions to literature and his unaffected preferences and opinions.

We talked in the café until after twelve and then we walked about half a mile to find our host waiting for us at the door of the ground floor. He was a small man with a thin feminine voice and had attended the lecture though I did not know that. We went up and up and up some four or five flights of stairs until we reached the last floor, where was our host's flat. As soon as you reached the last steps your eye was caught by a splendid piece of tapestry so large that it had to be put on the wall of the staircase. There was no room big enough to take it—one of those long pieces crammed with figures each one worth looking at. You saw that on the stairs and it struck the note of the rooms which followed. But first remember that I had never seen the man before, and I am pretty certain that the other two had not seen my Indian friend before either; neither had I seen my Indian friend more than once before. But we sat down between twelve and one in the morning to a first-class supper, course after course, as thick as thieves.

Our host took his place at the head of the table, joined in the conversation, moved round and got rid of dirty plates and shoved clean ones into their places, all in such an unobtrusive way that you would hardly take notice of it unless you were on the alert. One strange thing, however, was the entire absence of alcoholic drinks of any kind, and it is a peculiar thing to which I shall refer later but may mention in passing, how little the average middle-class English person seems to drink. And while we ate we talked. And the talk was good because our host's friend is a doctor of philosophy of Strasbourg University, an authority on art, architecture, music, ballet; is a lecturer on aesthetics; has been a colonel in the army; is only about fifty, and is as fit as nails, besides being one of the best chairmen that I have seen. When I say authority, I mean authority, for he writes criticism on these subjects for a well-known newspaper and signs his articles. Naturally he is a most delightful man to talk to. His friend had travelled in the East and naturally had a lot to say. He was also in his way an artist, for he showed us some beautiful decorative work done from toffee paper. Further, he was a man of unexpected parts. Every single thing on the table he had prepared himself. He gave me, by the way, some sugar cake, though he called it by another name, which was as good as anything I have eaten at home. He also had made all the curtains, the lampshades, and nearly all the screens round his whole flat of three or four rooms himself. Later he took us into his bedroom. It was a Chinese room. Every single thing in it was Chinese. The pictures on the walls, the decorations, the ornaments, the bedspread, Chinese; Chinese porcelain, Chinese rice paper, a gorgeous Chinese wedding garment, a Chinese hat, the room was in fact one mass of memories of China. There was profusion and yet, as far as I could see, order, if not symmetrical, yet governed by an instinctive good taste and sense of form. At last, after we had talked about all sorts of things and I had seen in particular a reproduction of some Pompeian wall paintings which I had heard about and wanted to see, my Indian friend and I left, somewhere about half past three to four. He had to go to a post office in Trafalgar Square in order to catch an air mail, but I had nothing to do and went home.

When I got up on Saturday morning I went down to the Times Book Club and spent an hour or two among the books and got an admirable history of British colonial policy with extracts of state papers, Trinidad figuring grandly with the rest, with among other things some dispatches from Lord Harris on the state of the island in the middle of the last century. The West African student had recommended to us Pirandello's *Six Characters in Search of an Author,* so I got the book there and went back home for lunch. I was by myself and lunch again was a hopeless failure. At about half past two, tired and sleepy but unable to sleep, I heard a knock at the door. "Two friends to see Mr. James," the maid said. I wondered who the devil they were but they turned out to be a man and his girl who had come to see me once before with another friend and who had liked me enough to come back. To tell the honest truth, I liked them immensely and was jolly glad to see them. The girl is very pretty, speaks very well, and this time was most charmingly dressed. The boyfriend is not at all good-looking, dresses even more carelessly than I do, but is in many respects one of the most stimulating and amusing men I have ever met. It would take pages to do justice to that fellow.

First of all we went for tea (to lay a foundation) and during tea the boyfriend told us all about Mussolini and the fascist regime. He had been to Italy and spoke Italian pretty fluently. Then we came back and the three of us went to a public house, whence we came out carrying three large bottles of beer and half a bottle of whisky. Between us we had about fifty cigarettes. Thus fortified we went into my room. I gave instructions that I was not to be disturbed and we sat down to talk. This was about half past three. We talked till ten and I was more lively at the end than I was at the beginning. My male visitor was a most provoking person. He accepted Mozart as indeed everyone does. He gave Beethoven a grudging respect. He abused Wagner unmercifully, but exalted Rossini and Verdi to the skies. But you could not help seeing that his admiration for Rossini and also Verdi was genuine, because every few minutes he would break out into snatches of well-known arias in the original Italian. His girl held more orthodox opinions and was on my side but there was no holding him. He was obviously accustomed to defending these indefensible positions and thrust and parried and skipped away to return to the attack in the most graceful and amusing way, so that it was impossible really to be annoyed with him. We agreed cordially that Thackeray was the greatest of English novelists, and drank a glass of beer to *The Pickwick Papers*.

At least I think it was *The Pickwick Papers.* Then we began to read passages from Shakespeare, matching passage for passage. We discovered a mutual disliking for Flecker's *Hassan,* and while I could quote verse, he went one better by quoting long passages of the prose, etc., etc., etc.

At ten o'clock the beer and the cigarettes were finished and it was time to do something. A typical Bloomsbury problem. What's to be done now. We would take a taxi and go to his room. I said no, I was tired, it was best for me to go to bed, but I would walk with them to the taxi rank. When we reached the girl got in and we shook hands. "Good night," I said. "Oh come along, come along with us," she replied. "No, I think I had better go back home," I said. "Oh come along, oh come with us please," still holding my hand, and with the boyfriend pushing me in from behind and the girlfriend pulling me in from in front, I went in. We reached his room at about eleven. To do what? Not a blessed thing but to sit before a fire and talk and read again. He read me extracts from a book by Mr. Gilbert Frankau and proved to me what I would not have believed, that Mr. Frankau is a man of real high spirits which frequently almost achieve wit and humour. On his shelf was also Edmund Rostand's *Cyrano de Bergerac* in the original French. I started to read the famous speech on his nose. My good friend went ahead with me line for line without the book. Then he in turn read the "Non merci" speech with immense vim and gusto; then he stretched himself on the floor and read me a short story which he had written—a tale of about fifteen hundred words: taut, wicked, scintillating. I laughed so much that I nearly fell over backwards. I have heard many things read during the last few weeks here, but this certainly was the star performance. Many more will laugh at that story some day. By this time we were hungry. I had a perfectly good dinner at home and so, I am sure, did the girl, but the boyfriend went off and brought back bread and butter and sardines and olives and we had a late supper which disappeared in no time.

By about half past one I had had enough and insisted on going home. I left them there, caught the last bus, and was home near two o'clock. When I reached home someone had dropped a letter in the box telling me to come over on Sunday morning between eleven and twelve because she would be at home then. I went, we went for lunch, went to the Student Movement House and read magazines and talked about them between four and eight, and then six of us met in her room and read Pirandello's *Six Characters in Search of an Author.* . . .

That is the sort of thing that is happening day after day. That is, of course, if you want it. If you want to go dancing you can. The opportunities are always there. Or if you want to go drinking you can also. The public houses are always there. But if you want to live the intellectual life Bloomsbury is the place.

And now I have something to say, something which seems to run counter to the spirit of all that I have written. Let no one who wishes to write believe that all I have described is life. In one important sense it is not life at all. It is a highly artificial form of living and I would not be surprised if a great deal of what modern work suffers from is not to be traced to that very cause.

> *Will no one tell me what she sings?—*
> *Perhaps the plaintive numbers flow*
> *For old, unhappy, far-off things*

And battles long ago:
Or is it some more humble lay,
Familiar matter of to-day?
Some natural sorrow, loss, or pain
That has been, and may be again?

Wordsworth did not learn to write like that by running about in Bloomsbury or any other literary quarter talking about books and art and music. These things come from deeper down. When you lie in bed in the early morning and have not slept and know that you will not sleep because of something you have to do the next day or someone you have to meet; or wish that you would never get up but go to sleep and sleep for ever; or think over your present position and feel how fine it is and wish that it would continue as it is: these things are the basis of life and of great writing and of great art in any part of the world. You get into contact with them by emotional relationships with people and with things and by communion with your own soul. They are the essentials. But also you require a knowledge of things, of the form and practice of art, and that the Bloomsbury atmosphere can give you. But that is, I repeat, secondary. At any rate, apart from all literary theory, the facts are as I have related them. That is the way I lived for four days. That is the way thousands of young students in their various ways are living. And that is my main impression of Bloomsbury, London, the intellectual ferment of the place.

In later articles I shall discuss other aspects, but I had better warn the reader that in order to appreciate them properly he must remember that I have seen the rest of London from the Bloomsbury background. Even though I see the Bloomsbury life for the secondary thing that it is, nevertheless both by instinct and by training I belong to it and have fit into it as naturally as a pencil fits into a sharpener. Birds of a feather will flock together.

The Houses

(Originally published in
the *Port of Spain Gazette*,
27 July, 1932)

I want to describe the average lodging house where the students, large numbers of middle-class people, especially those who are not married, and a good number of visitors live. The best way is to describe the lodging house where I live, right in the centre of London with hundreds of other houses all round me of much the same type.

Now I have often noticed in reading that although the writer has taken much trouble to describe a room of a house or a structure of some kind, yet he has been able to make no impression on my mind. To avoid this I shall do my best to be very explicit.

To begin with, the house is not a house at all but a set of rooms in one big house. I lived at No. 14. But from No. 1 to the next corner, all the houses were joined together. You could only look out of the window to the front if you had a front room, or to the back if you had a back room. You could not look out at the side anywhere, because the side of one house was the side of the other. I now have quite a tolerable idea of what it must feel like to be in gaol. But to begin at the beginning.

The pavement on our side of the street is about six feet broad. Let us say that we are going to No. 14 and we stand in front of it. Take a first glimpse from the pavement. The house is about sixteen feet broad, not an inch more, the whole house, mind you, and it is about sixty feet high. Just windows and walls, windows and walls, windows and walls right up to the top story. You look at No. 12. It is the same thing. You look at No. 16. It is the same thing. From one end of the street to the other, one long row of buildings all joined together, or, rather, one long building equally divided into numbered bits. Let us go inside.

To go inside we have to cross over a bridge about three feet or less in length, which makes the house about nine feet in all from the edge of the road. But the bridge by which we pass is very narrow and the space between the one bridge and the other bridge is empty. You can look right down and on the opposite side there are steps leading down to the basement. For it is down there that the landlady and her family live. But we'll come to them later.

You press a bell and the door is opened. You are invited to come in, that is to say, if at the first sight of you and your colour the door is not slammed in your face, or the landlady says that she is full, or she tells you quite frankly that she does not take coloured men, or she says very rudely that she wants no black men. Well, you go in and you stand in a passage. This passage is not one inch wider than three feet and I doubt if it is as much.

Personally, I think that two feet is a good average. Now remember that the whole house is sixteen feet wide. The passage takes up two feet, and the door being to one side, and not in the centre, we have the first room on the right, about fourteen feet square. Get it carefully please. The house sixteen feet wide, a passage to one side about two feet in width. And to one side, in this case the right, the first room.

Facing you in the passage are two staircases, one going up, and one going down. But at the side of these two staircases and behind the front room, they have managed to squeeze in a small room about eight feet square. Those two rooms, the passage and the beginning of the staircases constitute what is known as the ground floor. Let us go up the staircase, which is no wider than the passage. You go up twelve steps and then turn back and go up another ten. Then you come to a landing-place, for two rooms, one covering not the fourteen feet square of the first room on the ground floor, but the sixteen feet, for the two feet belonging to the passage are now included in the room. There is the same little room tacked on behind. Up you go another set of steps and two more rooms, the big one in front and the little one behind. Up you go another set of steps to two more rooms, another one in front and a little one behind. Up you go another set of steps and then you come to three rooms each very small. You can go no further for the roof is above your head. That is the whole house. Now what beats me completely is, not that poor old women have to rent these places and sublet for a living, but that these houses were built early in the nineteenth century, some of them, as dwelling houses for families. As dwelling houses for families which were fairly well-to-do. One characteristic of the English people, even the most confirmed city-dwellers, is their love for the country, their love for the open air. It is not difficult to understand, however. How a man could build such a prison for himself to live in or having a little money consent to live in one is beyond my understanding. This is not a rash judgment. Nobody builds that type of house today. But there they are and there they will remain until after the next war when modern flats will replace them if there is anybody left to build them or when they are built to live in them.

Let us finish with the house. The staircase which led downwards took you into the basement, two rooms. One the kitchen, the other the living room for the landlady, her husband and three or four children, an aunt or two and a few friends, according to taste. The maid lives in one of the rooms at the top. When families dwelt in these houses the servants occupied the little rooms at the top. And these rooms or at least some of them had no fireplaces because servants were not supposed to feel cold and increase the expense of their masters. At least that is what I am told. To complete the picture, at the back of the landing-place on the ground floor where the two staircases begin are the out offices, lavatory, and the unfrequented bathroom. There is a yard about eight inches square. That is the house complete. Of course there are varieties. I preferred to describe one that I know well. I should say that very probably five hundred thousand, perhaps a million people are living in rooms in houses of that type all over London. Some are better. A good many are worse.

Now imagine yourself in one of these rooms. There is only one exit, the door. There are windows to the front, if you have a front room, and there are windows to the back if you have a back room. But you open the top of the window to get a little fresh air. You don't open it to see outside, because there is nothing to see except the opposite side of the road, one long building from corner to corner, divided into houses same as yours, nothing else but windows and walls, windows and walls, from top to bottom. That is to the front. If you have a back room you have the view of your neighbours' back yard, or the tops of the buildings next to you; that is, if you are rather high up. If you are low down you may get a few square yards of wall and are lucky if you get nothing worse.

In the room itself, it is not so bad. According to your landlady you may have a few good chairs, a good bed etc. If you furnish it yourself, you may do quite well. But whatever you do the loneliness of the room is dreadful. When you lock the door you are in a world of your own. You come in, you pass along the passage, you go up the staircase, you go into your room, and there is an end of you. You see no one, you hear no one. You see nothing, all that you hear is the cry of newsboys, or vehicles passing along the street. Who are living in the same house with you, you do not know. Your landlady brings your meals or sends them by the maid into your room. Often the girls do their meals themselves and, as the rooms are tidied after you have gone, these girls need not even see the landlady. Oscar Ribeiro (who by the way has done wonderfully well for himself at London University) was in the same lodging house with me for six days and I did not know until I met him quite by accident in the passage one day. We might have lived there for three months and never seen each other. It is when you appreciate what this means that you see why there is a cinema or a theatre or a show of some kind every fifty yards in a London street. The million or two who have no homes in the strict sense of the term want to get out. They don't want to stay in those rooms, not under any circumstances. To work all day and then come home to that would kill a normal person in five years. So he or she comes in and then, unless there is work to be done, goes off somewhere else, anywhere, anywhere, out of the room. How the girls stand it I do not know. But as a matter of fact I do know. They do not stand it. They go out. They are always willing to go out, always willing. Those who have intellectual interests have a better chance. They have books, music and the resources of their own minds with which to employ themselves. But the average shop girl depends for happiness on the boyfriend. He will take her to the pictures. But if he can't afford to pay for two, she will pay for herself and think nothing of it. If they can't afford to go to the pictures, then he comes to see her or she goes to see him. But stick in that room by herself, she will not. And she is right. So determined she is, not to, that when there is not a regular boyfriend on hand she will take up with anyone passing. Sometimes you will see her sitting in a café, dawdling over a meal. When she is finished she reads the paper from cover to cover. I sit in the corner and watch her. If you ask her to go to the cinema with you and you look all right, she will take a chance and go. And it seems to me one reason is that she will do anything rather than work from nine till six and then go and lock herself away from the world in that prison of a room. But I am anticipating matters.

* * * *

Of course that is not the whole story. Even in these dreadful lodging houses you will find many girls with woman's natural instinct, and the opportunities which London gives, making a fine room out of this unpleasant material. She will have a divan on which friends can sit during the day and on which she sleeps at night. The pillows and the bed-clothes are all skilfully hidden away. You see a cabinet in a corner. It is a washstand containing all sorts of things. Although she may cook meals in the room, there is a neat little box by the side of the fireplace into which everything goes. She will have her own pictures, she will have her own wallpaper and her own curtains, making her own colour scheme. She will buy flowers, sixpence a time, and place them about the room. Now and then, you will see a book stand with an admirable bunch of books. She will have her own gramophone. The records, however, are usually tripe. That is the younger generation at its best. The men are usually Philistines.

When you go out to private houses in the suburbs, there is a different story. Of course, the climate is such that they have to build close and not open as in the tropics. There is also the terrible habit of joining all the houses one to another for hundreds of yards and very often building them according to a certain design, but all of the same design. So that a man who has had a glass or two extra must be in some trouble to find his own particular doorway where every house is the exact replica of every other house. But inside these houses, the few I have been into, I have been astonished by the standard of comfort. The rooms are all beautifully papered, if even the pattern of the paper is sometimes horrible. There is usually a piano, if even they play badly. There are large and finely upholstered chairs, divans, cushions, rugs so that you can sit on the floor, a good bookcase if even it holds rubbishy books, which often is not the case, now and then an original oil painting or watercolour, sometimes an etching. Here, in general arrangement and regard for comfort and appearance combined, they have our people, of a corresponding class, beaten to bits. Of course things are cheaper in London, but even making all allowances, the home looks a far more comfortable place and a place over which far more care is taken than the average middle-class home in Trinidad. I have not been to many, because I preferred the company of Bloomsbury people. Furthermore, fidgeting about with teacups and bits of cake, and saying how many lumps I took, and all that sort of business, bored me stiff. But the few times I went were enough to show me that the English people have been living many more centuries than we have and have learned a thing or two during that time.

Finally, these houses do not seem anything so difficult to run as ours are. The kitchen in a modern house is a marvel of cleanliness and labour-saving devices. Now the average wife, having despatched her husband to work, will not see him again until long after six. For he usually takes lunch outside. She is finished with what she has to do quite early in the forenoon. It is my firm belief that women, not having to provide for men, would never cook a decent meal for themselves except about once a month. The result is, they have the whole day on their hands. Not a single thing to do. That is the kind of person with whom Satan has little difficulty. So we have the two of them shaped by circumstances: the lonely inhabitant of the prison, after working all day, seeking distraction of any kind rather than staying at home; and the young woman or the woman approaching middle age, who is in fairly decent circumstances, with no children or perhaps one, with nothing to do in a modern house. They are the most interesting phenomena of the place to me, these women. They fill the cinemas, from twelve in the day to twelve at night, seeking vicariously or intensifying their restless craving for excitement. They are modern. They are urban—a bad combination. Emancipated. They have their liberty, but they don't know what to do with it. They buy the evening papers, but not to read about Lausanne or Geneva, but about the Rector of Stiffkey. Anything, anywhere out of that room. A man can stand it. A man will stand anything. He will join the army and march, left, right, left, right, for twenty years and be happy, or at least not unhappy. But women have a greater sense of the realities of life than men. They trust to their instincts, which is more trustworthy than the reasoning of the half-educated. And they do what they feel to do—get at any price. I know what I am talking about. I have seen it. And then, you see, I myself in one of those dreadful rooms have felt the same.

The Men

(Originally published in
the *Port of Spain Gazette*,
4 August, 1932)

I shall begin by relating what I have been assured and have every reason to believe is a perfectly true story. Two Englishmen took the train from a suburb every morning and sat opposite one another in the same compartment. When they got in they arranged overcoats—or rather blew their noses, arranged overcoats, blew their noses again, lit up and read the newspaper. This they did for six years, but never having been introduced, never spoke to one another. After six years, it happened that they took their holiday the same week. Unknown to each other, they both decided to go to France. One day they met in Paris, face to face. They looked at each other. Then each, I suppose, remembered that he was an Englishman. Each turned aside and went his way.

Speak when you are spoken to.

And answer when you are called.

That by way of preliminary.

I am going to give a few isolated shots. The reader will be able to build up his general impressions. I say his general impressions, advisedly. In forming judgements on so wide a subject, one has to go slowly.

One day I walked into a bookshop to buy

a couple of French magazines. A girl, a pretty girl, with her hair most delightfully done, and her fingernails most abominably black, a not unusual combination, spread them out before me, heaps and heaps—in fact, all except the particular two I wanted. I was speaking English, and, if I may say so, quite good English. A woman of about forty, dressed in black, came into the shop. She stood looking at some magazines for a while and then when the shop assistant turned her back, she came up to me and spoke in French. Did I read French a lot? As much as I could. Where did I come from? *La Trinité—les Antilles Britanniques.* Was I staying in London a long time? Yes. For some years, I thought. Did I hope to visit France someday? Yes, I very much hoped to. That was very nice. I smiled appreciatively. Goodbye. Goodbye. A slight but quite charming episode. But please note that she was a Frenchwoman.

Now see what happened on another day. I stood in the Strand with a map in my hand, trying to find out exactly how certain streets went. It may have looked strange. I didn't care. London is a blessed place where you need not care. I knew where I was, and I knew where I was going, but I wished to place myself well in my own mind with a view to future wanderings in the same quarter. So I stood at the corner and with map and pencil did a little astronomy or whatever is the proper name for it. Then I became aware of a man about twelve feet away who was peeping at me out of the corner of his eye. He was over fifty, a short fellow, clean-shaven, with a healthy red face and a very pleasant well-meaning look. He was obviously peeping at me, so while I busied myself with my map I had a peep at him. His behaviour was most curious. He had a peep and then he looked round, then he sidled towards me about a foot or so. Then he looked at the roadway, he looked at me, and he sidled towards me another foot. When he had done that twice I put the map away and looked at him rather suspiciously. By this time he had decided to do what he wanted to do. He came up to me. Was there anywhere I wanted to find?

The poor man had wanted all the time to offer his services. But whether he thought I could not understand English, or whether he thought I would bark at him and bite him if he spoke to me, I do not know. I believe that he behaved as he did for the same reason that those two who travelled in the train for six years would not speak to each other, even when they met in Paris. I had nowhere to go in particular, but I gave him some fictitious address, and we walked along together. He pointed out one or two places to me on the way, directed me carefully to the post office I asked him for, and then told me goodbye. He was not a rogue, pickpocket or anything of the kind. He behaved as he did because he was an Englishman. The contrast between his discomfort and the easy, pleasant manner of the Frenchwoman was vast.

Let me give another isolated shot.

I used to frequent a café, the Russell Square tube café, and I do not want to start to talk about that café at all, because I would never stop. I sat usually right down at the back with my back to the wall, so that I could see all that was happening in front. One night I noticed a man sitting just opposite to me. He looked at me and I looked at him. The next night, I had a rather long discussion about colonial administration with a West African and an Abyssinian. My friend was in the corner again. He had his paper before him, but I could see that he was listening closely. The next night, we got into conversation. He offered me matches or something. I used to meet him fairly often after that and we used to talk. He was a man in business, rather an important business too, a firm with a very well known name, and his name was on their note paper. He was a young fellow, in the middle thirties I would say, with a delicate, refined, very handsome face. I used to tell him about the West Indies. He used to tell me about business in England. He was not very well educated, at least in the academic sense of the term. He had come from below, but he had made the best use of his opportunities, and though I have met some clever men here, I have met few men who spoke so well. It was nothing for us to talk for an hour or two, and he put me wise about many things in the business world of London.

Well, then, one night he told me that he was taking a midnight train to one of the biggest towns in England to meet the representatives of a certain firm. He was going to put through a deal which might mean thirty thousand pounds to his firm and maybe a thousand pounds for himself. He had been to the Continent some six or seven times to make sure of all his facts. He put them before me. I asked him lots of questions. Then he drew from his pocket the prospectus which he was going to use as the basis of his attack the next day, and asked me to look it over, and point out to him anything which I noticed out of place or ill-sounding. I was taken a bit by surprise. But I looked through and pointed out a few things. From that we went on to discuss literature and writing, which we had discussed now and then before. It got late, we became more intimate, and at last I gathered that my friend was not too confident about his interview of the morrow. He confessed to me that he was always a bit uncertain of himself when he had to meet and speak to groups of people. His education— I told him that I didn't see what he had to be nervous about, he spoke as well as most people whom I had met, and if he spoke to boards of directors or to people of any kind as he spoke to me, I didn't see that he had anything to be afraid of. I told him that in these matters I was rather critical and a bit of a judge myself. But I must confess that his attitude had me a bit surprised. We talked on, but he still harped on his uncertainty for the next day, and at last he blurted out the truth:

"You see, a good many of those fellows whom I am going to meet tomorrow are titled men, Lord So-and-so, Sir So-and-so O.B.E., and lots of them have been to Oxford and Cambridge—"

The thing came as a violent shock to me.

The man was master of his subject. He had taken an enormous amount of trouble to be quite sure of all his facts. He spoke admirably, not only on this particular business, but on all sorts of subjects that cropped up. And yet, here he was nervous and shaking because the men he would have to speak to were lords and had titles, and had been to Oxford and Cambridge. The reader need not accept it from me. But I believe that is a particularly English characteristic. You meet it all over the place and in the most unexpected quarters. I remember one day talking to a man, a West Indian, a magnificent pianist, well known in the musical world of London. He was talking of how sometimes you meet people who would help you on towards the realisation of your aims. And he mentioned So-and-so, who was the cousin of Lord So-and-so. Not Sir Henry Wood, mark you, nor Sir Landon Ronald, nor Mr. Ernest Newman, nor Mr. Frederick Lamond, nor anybody big in the musical world, but Mr. So-and-so, who was a cousin of Lord So-and-so. And I dare say the man who said it was quite right in his point of view.

It is a thing I have noticed also in Trinidad with English people. More than any creole, white or black, they lose their heads at the prospect of contact with the great. I remember one of the finest Englishmen I have ever known, Mr. William Burslem, getting so excited one morning that I don't think he knew his right hand from his left, and simply because the Governor had sent to say that on his way down to work he would pass in for a visit of a few minutes. I was a small boy at the time, but I saw it and remembered distinctly being puzzled over it for quite a while. The Governor was coming. You had to give orders that everything was to be ship-shape. You would meet him at the gate and bow and say that it was an honour and a pleasure, and carry him round and introduce him, and tell all the boys that it was an honour and a pleasure. And thank him graciously for the half holiday and say that it was an honour and a pleasure, and then bid him goodbye, bowing in the proper way, while assuring him that his visit was indeed an honour and a pleasure. But why should there have been all this running up and down the stairs, and putting on the gown, and putting on the cap, and taking the cap off again, and running to classrooms, and giving orders, and conferring with masters, and standing in the passage with hand to eyes gazing into the distance to see if the carriage with the policemen out-riding was coming, with almost the same intentness that the sailors of Columbus looked for land, all this I could not understand then and, I must say, cannot understand now. But if they do a lot of it in the Colonies, the English do quite a lot of it at home. You see it everywhere.

I cannot make this article too long. But here is one subject which I must refer to. And that is colour prejudice. The average Englishman in London is, on the surface, quite polite. Furthermore, you will make friends with certain people or even certain families and they will stick by the average coloured man and even quarrel with some of their friends who treat him in any out-of-the-way manner, and generally prove themselves staunch with a staunchness that is particularly English. But nevertheless the average man in London is eaten up with colour prejudice. This is a big subject and I am going to tackle it someday in the way it deserves. Meanwhile, here are three more shots.

I have been to two dances here. There

were heaps of nice girls, really nice people, well-educated, good manners, and some of them quite beautifully dressed. Who thinks that the average coloured student has to associate with barmaids, shabby waitresses and that type is very much mistaken. He associates with them only if he wants to, or if he carries himself in such a way that only persons of that type will take any notice of him. But there were very few English *men* there. Those present were either connected with the giving of the dance, or friends of those who had given it. At one dance in particular there were no more than about five men under thirty, one might almost say under fifty. And these five sat in corners and glowered, and looked as unpleasant and as dissatisfied as possible. That tells its own tale.

For another, even more significant.

One night I got into the last tube at a crowded station. The train was waiting for a while and I sat in a corner reading. I lifted my eyes quite by chance and through the glass door caught the eye of a girl who was standing on the platform waiting for another train. She was not particularly good-looking, but she was tall with a good figure and had a very healthy red face. So, manlike, I began to read my paper, but took a slight squint over the top of it. I noticed that the young lady was engaged in the same game, but womanlike, in a way not quite as discreet as mine. Two people cannot peep at one another for any length of time without bouncing, so to speak. Our eyes met fairly and she smiled a bit. I dropped my paper and we looked at one another in a friendly sort of way. A friend of hers was near, reading a paper. She gave the friend a dig in the ribs with an elbow. The friend looked up. They both had a look. And started to giggle. They were not common women. I dare say they were only having a little fun with a strange man and enjoying themselves in their own way. It didn't worry me. The train started to move out. They smiled more and more and I gave them a grave bow and a faint smile by way of goodbye, at which they laughed more than ever. But before I got back to my paper, I was attracted by the strange antics of an Englishman sitting next to me. This fellow, it seemed, had seen all that had taken place. What business it was of his, I do not know. But as the train moved off, he glared and glared at the girls and shuffled his feet, and glared at me, and looked me up from head to foot, and squirmed and twisted like a man suffering from an acute attack of dysentery or colitis. Friends of mine had warned me, and I could recognise his symptoms. He was a chronic sufferer from colour prejudice. The idea that an English girl would smile at a negro almost drove him mad. And it is a characteristic of large numbers of Englishmen. On the other hand, men who have been to France say that the average Frenchman no more looks at you than he would look at a very tall or a very short man.

This man I could afford to ignore. Sometimes, however, these interfering wretches cannot be so easily dismissed, and can make life very unpleasant.

I brought a letter of introduction to a girl in London from a friend at home. I carried it to her and none of my own people could have given me a warmer welcome. Any friend of ——— she was only too glad to see. How was he? How was his wife? Anyway, more of that later. One night we went out and coming home together stood up in a lift. In the lift with us was an Englishman, an ordinary, middle-class, commonplace Englishman. There are millions like him all round you in London every day, the kind of person I would not walk five yards out of my way to meet, except for the sake of curiosity and to find out what was in his *Daily Express*, cinema-fed mind. But he, this Anglo-Saxon member of a ruling race, despised me to such an extent that he could not contain his wrath at seeing me with a girl who was not from the street. He chewed at his cigarette and looked round and stared at the girl as if to say, "You ought to be ashamed of yourself for going about with this fellow." There was another woman in the lift whose eyes and general demeanour said much the same thing. And they were not the only two, although they were the two most obstreperous. The girl told me afterwards that she saw quite well, but it is a thing that girls who got out with coloured men have to be prepared for. Some day, as I have said, I am going to strip this question raw of all the cant and hypocrisy with which it is covered today. The fault, by the way, is not all on the English side. Not by any means. But when every allowance is made, there remains something in the average Englishman which can only be called sheer, blind prejudice. It is a commonplace among students. Often you meet people who are quite cordial. India, West India, East Indies, West Indies, they are for the most part very hazy about. Often curiosity makes them anxious to know you. An Englishman is always willing to add a few facts to his store. It is ideas that beat him. He makes your acquaintance. He is agreeably surprised. Come to lunch. Come to tea. This is my wife, my daughter. This is Miss X. This is Miss Y. Charmed. Delighted. So happy. Very, very pleased. But let him see you sitting in the park talking with Miss X. That is another story. An Englishman can cause any scandal. German, Frenchman, South African, Canadian. "What a pity! Rascal," they say, and leave it at that. But let Mr. Black Man beware. Go to France, to Spain, to Italy, I am told. Carry yourself like a gentleman, you'll be treated as one. But in England watch your step and, however much at home you feel, watch it in this particular direction.

So much for the present. The next article will be on the girls.

The Women

(Originally published in
the *Port of Spain Gazette*,
11 August, 1932)

In an earlier article I spoke about a letter of introduction. On the day after I reached London I carried it to the person to whom it was addressed, someone working in a firm in the City. The young lady read it and said, "I see. From So-and-so. Well, it's rather awkward here. Where are you staying?"

I said where I was staying.

"I leave work at six and will come over by seven. Will that suit you?"

Yes, it would.

"Very well then, at seven or perhaps a little later."

Punctually at seven, she turned up and started to talk as easily as if we had known each other all our lives, and not making conversation in the dreadfully boring way that some people do, but just talking; about people whom we both knew, about what I had come to London to do, about her work, about her people, about my people. Two men with whom I had travelled over and who were staying in the same house came in and we had a general conversation. Then they cleared off. We stayed talking and talking until maybe about half past ten. There were certain things I had to get and, as I am always robbed whenever I go to buy anything, it had been suggested that she should help me, especially as she had facilities. She found out what I wanted, measured me capably, and then said that she would bring along samples on Monday evening. I protested against this extravagance of good will. In vain. On Monday evening she turned up with the stuff, stuff admirable in every way, and saving me in all some forty or fifty per cent of the cost. After that, I usually saw her about once a week. She dared not take me home. Her people would have got fits. And then worse still she was engaged to be married. From photographs and from what she told me, he was a real true blue son of Britain who might break the engagement on the spot.

It was a good introduction to English women in London. She was pretty, she was tidy; she was not intellectual, far from it, but she spoke well. Best of all she was very much at home, very very much at home, in fact just at the start far more at home than I was. That is what I admired in her chiefly, her independence, her ease, her total lack of constraint. They have a lot of freedom, these girls. They go where they like, when they like, merely sending home to say as a matter of politeness where they are.

Over and over again, I have seen girls go to a public telephone and telephone home to say that they are going to So-and-so's and not coming home for the night. They go off to France or Germany or the country districts of England on parties with men, four girls and four men. Or sometimes she and the boyfriend and maybe two others will take a holiday together. The result is that the average young woman has got rid, for the most part, of male complexes. I dare say in some respects she has lost, but the gain in ordinary intercourse is immense. That girl was easy with me in a manner impossible to the average young woman brought up under different circumstances.

There is another type, the student type approximating somewhat to the Bloomsbury girl. She inclines to the Bohemian. Quite often she has had a good education, much the same education as a man has had. The mere fact that she is on her own denotes or at least means that she will have acquired some sort of independence of mind and judgement. She reads as widely and her judgements of books, of music, of painting, are as sound as those of the average man in the same group. Often she spends more money and time on these things than he does. She is awfully good company; though, from my point of view at any rate, too much inclined to be careless about clothes. About public opinion she has a fine scorn, and will knock at your window at about half past ten or eleven on her way home and come in and stay till one without turning a hair. Her main preoccupation is that men treat her, or at least most men should treat her, as an individual and not as a woman in the Victorian sense of the word. Some of them carry it to lengths. They will not allow you to carry a bag for them. Why should you carry it, is their point. You are you and I am me. You carry your bag and I will carry mine. If I have two you will help me with one. But then if you have two, I will help you with one just the same. No favours required from men, please. Some of them won't even allow themselves to be taken out. They will go but they will pay. You work for your money and I work for mine. And so on. I got to know a few girls of this type, or approaching it, and they were very good company, very good company indeed. Despite all their masculinity, they were nevertheless women, although it would rather annoy them to be told that. But they were very quick, full of humour, far more

humour, strange to say, than the average man.
And I look back on many conversations, with
ideas, and very interesting ideas too, floating
about the place, from people who had read quite
a few books which I had not, whose actual
experience of English conditions was so
immeasurably superior to mine, and who
nevertheless preserved a certain grace and
delicacy which is peculiar to women, and is
usually absent from masculine company.
Somehow I remember with them too an
immense amount of laughing. And it was
strange, because the conversations were rarely
frivolous. D.H. Lawrence, Bolshevik Russia, sex,
the Indian question, British Imperialism,
Abyssinia, coloured students in London, the
English people, and yet it is surprising the
amount of liveliness that came from these
questions. I remember a desert island (in the
West Indies or the South Seas) to which some
of us, being thoroughly sick of the world, were
to go. It came up for discussion often. We went
into detail. We discussed all possibilities. It was
carried unanimously that there would be
sanctuaries scattered all over the island and
whoever reached a sanctuary was for the time
being safe. And then one man asked if there

were not to be sanctuaries for men also. If there were not, he wasn't coming.

One thing about most of these girls is that they are not stand-offish or exclusive. In Bloomsbury in particular you will meet all sorts. The intellectuals do not despise the ordinary shop girl and there is not that horrible exclusiveness which kills so much of our social life in Trinidad. All that they seem to ask of you is that you be not dull.

But even these are not the normal type. In a previous article I have already hinted at the average girl working in a bookshop, draper's shop, bureau of some sort, the million and one occupations which London offers, the girl who lives by herself, or, even if she lives at home, has an unattractive home and goes her own way. Salaries are not high. I saw an article the other day which stated that she works for about twenty-five shillings a week very often, sometimes more, but not too much more. You see her in the streets or in the cafés, shoes and stockings always very fine, and clean, which cannot always be said of her brother. Her hair is always very well done. They are as careful about it as they are of the shoes and stockings. After that most of their difficulty is over, because they usually wear a coat. A good coat gives a finish and they are not in half so much trouble about the dresses as they would be if they lived in the tropics. Even in the heart of the city, their complexions are usually very good, and they carry to a fine art the wearing of scarves and caps to match their complexions. Sometimes, for example, you see a girl whose face is all red and white, with very fair hair. She has her hair done so that it is shining in the sun. And she means you to see it because she is wearing a little cap about four inches square just stuck on the back of her head. The cap is red, dead red, matching her complexion. The scarf also maybe red and white. And the general effect is quite stunning. And as the complexions and hair vary so do caps and scarves and sometimes even coats. It is all very interesting to watch.

They are always in a hurry, going to work or coming from work or going to lunch or coming from lunch or going to meet the boyfriend or hurrying along with him somewhere. You should see them running along and hopping on the buses or dashing down tubes. A girl will run twenty yards, with a bag in one hand, shoulder you out of the way, and take a flying leap at a bus moving off, in a way that would do credit to many an athlete. They have to see after themselves. Young men do not give way to them, do not stand aside for them to pass, do not give them seats in crowded vehicles, with the result that men and these young women scramble and jostle in a way that I personally find quite strange. But the young women don't. They are prepared for it.

All people are out for a good time, but this type in particular is. I have been told, though I have not seen it myself, that in the big towns there are districts where some of these girls congregate, waiting for motorcyclists to come along. Please remember that these are not girls of the street. But they will do anything rather than sit at home. So they stand at the corners and the cyclists come up and give them a wink. They reply in the affirmative. Up they go behind and he goes off. I am told too that many a man has found his wife in this way. The cyclist, by the way, is not looking for a woman of the street. If he wanted one he could find one easily enough. He is looking for a girl to go out with. She is looking for a boyfriend. They may like each other and then decide to meet again and again. I remember a phrase of O. Henry's, "a girl has got to meet the men." He cannot come knocking at strange lodging houses. So she is on the alert to catch any unattached swain. You see them sometimes sitting in restaurants, where they have rushed in for lunch or for tea, sometimes from work. Two girls sometimes. You and another man are sitting not too far off. They order their sausages and mash, or roast beef and Yorkshire pudding, and sit waiting. Watch them closely. Their eyes are dancing with excitement. Every move is an invitation. Experienced youths tell you that all you have to do is go over, start a conversation, and ask them to go to the pictures that evening. Of course you run a risk of being snubbed, but if you look respectable, by which I mean a decent sort of person, they are quite willing. You arrange where you will meet and off you go to the cinema. The acquaintance may develop. It may not. It does not matter. She is a working girl. But one thing she will not do without is her boyfriend. Life moves quickly and she has to catch him as he passes. I haven't had much to do with girls of this type, in fact have merely talked to them when I met them in company with others of a different type. Doubtless all this freedom must result in a lot of licence. But though I have had little means of judging, still I doubt if this constant going out together means what the average person in Trinidad is likely to think it means. It is a difficult subject. I leave it alone. I have my own ideas but my data is horribly insufficient.

And now for a side view on the question of colour. The average English girl in London has little colour prejudice, and in fact were it not for English men I doubt if she would have any at all. When I say the average, I mean the Bloomsbury type or the average working girl with whom most of the young men, white and coloured, who live alone associate. I have not been here a long time, it is true, but I have talked to lots of men, and I have used my eyes. The girls, far from being prejudiced, are very much interested, but they are afraid of public opinion, and no one can blame them. But judging from the way they look and look and look, and from what many other coloured students have told me, it is the men who are responsible for a great deal of the trouble. In my short experience I have met too many instances of English women, English girls of decent upbringing and education, who have gone out of their way to help in every way they could young men of colour in London. I am

not speaking of any boyfriend and girlfriend
business, or love affairs, or anything of the sort.
I mean pure and simple friendship, genuine
good will, and a desire to help the stranger in a
foreign land. Furthermore, any man of colour
who is not repulsive in appearance, has good
manners, and is fairly intelligent, is a great
favourite with the girls. It is since I have come
here that I have learned to appreciate the good
qualities of West Indians. The average West
Indian in a group lacks solidarity. He is not
strong on the race question or on imperialism
as the West Africans or the Ceylonese or the
Indians are. But compared with the other
nationalities, he is a most charming fellow, and
the girls like him immensely. If I were a girl, I
would myself. For the English native is so dull
and glum and generally boorish in his manners,
that the girls turn with relief from these dreadful
Englishmen to the smiling and good-natured
West Indians. At which the Englishman sits in
a corner and scowls and makes himself as
unpleasant as possible. Yet, on the other hand,
there is something to be said from the English
point of view, which resents the comparative
lack of prejudice of the normal London girl.
Coloured men are supposed to be loose in their

general character and their association with English girls is supposed to bode no good for the girl. You only have to live in this country for a fortnight to know exactly how vast an amount of smoke there is and how small an amount of fire in the statement. How hypocritical such a statement is. But nevertheless there is something in it. And I can best illuminate by giving an experience of my own.

I went to the theatre one night with another coloured man. I sat down and did not look towards my left. But suddenly my arm on the chair was touched by another arm. I looked round and saw a girl sitting with her boyfriend, his arm around her, and both of them very close together. I moved my arm away and went on looking at the picture. Five minutes after, arm on arm again. A little later, elbow in my ribs. A little later, ankle against mine. By this time I was thoroughly alarmed. If the man next to her got any idea of what was happening, she would most certainly say that I was doing it. Which would have meant perhaps a first-class row and unpleasantness which I was anxious to avoid. I pulled myself away and turned round to have a glimpse at this intruder on my peace. By this time she had disengaged herself from the arm of her friend. But he, poor fellow, was still holding her hand tightly, though intent on the picture. When I turned to look at her she turned to look at me. She was between eighteen and twenty-two, a blonde, and extremely pretty. She looked up at me and smiled. But I wasn't having any and pulled arm and foot resolutely away. No good, ten minutes after they were up against mine again where they stayed until the end of the show. I dodged *God Save the King* and cleared out with my friend, so did not stay to see exactly who and what she was. The proper technique would have been to follow her and her unsuspecting young man. She would soon find out if her invitation had been accepted. If it had, she would have found it not difficult to shake off the Romeo in attendance—from what I could see of him, he was a dull, unpromising sort of person—and then, with him out of the way, there would have begun, as Rosalind says, new matter.

Now take a boy of eighteen, a coloured boy living in the colonies, where the social question is what we know it is. Drop him in London, to live on his own, with two hundred pounds a year to spend, and a few hours' work to do every day. He is at a critical age, the age when he is apt to believe that sex and a woman are one and the same thing—an age which many may never outgrow. Round him flutter red and white faces with blond hair, red caps and red and white scarves. Some of them pass him by, but some don't. They know what they want and do not hesitate to go straight for it. It is not surprising that some of the boys get spoilt. They do get spoilt. There is no doubt about it. Whence comes the fact that young John Bull sits in corners of trams or buses or at the theatre and eats his heart out when he sees one of his womankind making much of one of the lesser breeds without the law.

Here ends the third lesson. The next articles will be on less controversial matter. Meanwhile, let me state finally the fairly obvious, that my experience has been, comparatively speaking, very limited. For instance, I have not seen much of the really delicately bred upper-middle-class type. But I have met a few in Bloomsbury, and they are distinctive. Not more cultured than the Bloomsbury girls—much less so; but certainly they have a charming style and manner, a sort of refinement and dignity which the Bloomsbury girl has not—and, as far as I can see, rather despises. This type is difficult to know. They themselves don't mind but their people are usually the sort who object to all foreigners on principle. But one gets to know all things in time. So that these impressions are incomplete and disjointed. But as I wrote in the article on Barbados, one has impressions. One cannot help having them. I have tried as much as possible to avoid generalisation. All I can say is, I saw and heard these things and have written them or, rather, have dictated them. If only I could write I would have written far more comprehensively.

.

The Nucleus of a
Great Civilisation

(Originally published in
the *Port of Spain Gazette*,
28 August, 1932)

For the time being I shall draw this series of articles to a close. It is not that information is exhausted. Not at all. The streets of London, the food the people eat, their way of dress, their manners, by which I mean the way they behave to one another in public and in private, all these things I have found endlessly interesting. For the time being, however, I wish to sum up, so to speak, the impressions which I have been describing.

London is not England, but London is the peak, the centre, the nucleus of a great branch of western civilisation. It is the capital city of a country which has played a great part in the history of the world during the last few centuries. What exactly, as far as that can be put into words, did this civilisation register on me?

Well, to be frank, on the whole I was not impressed. Let me say why, in as clear a way as I can. Perhaps the fault is in myself. If that is so, it does not alter the fact that I was not impressed.

There are some simple people who are impressed by the traffic. I was not impressed by the traffic. To me the traffic was simply a nuisance and nothing else, because if you have eight million people pressed into a small space and the majority of them rushing hither and thither and sending goods and food and other things of the kind up and down the place then you cannot but expect a lot of traffic. If with all this activity there was little traffic then that would be wonderful indeed. Or if a small country town had all this vast amount of traffic then that would be still more wonderful. But that London, being what it is, should have a deal of traffic, is to me quite inevitable, only to be expected and, therefore, except to country bumpkins or people who make up their minds to admire, nothing to be wondered at.

Then there are the buildings. You walk along and there they are, very big, very massive, and, to one accustomed to our little shanties at home, they are at first sight very imposing. But walk along the streets for a few days. When the first novelty has worn off you begin to look at them critically. Few of them are beautiful. Some of the older dwelling houses are the most unlovely things you can set your eyes on—but I have described that already and there is no need to dilate any more on those. There are beautiful buildings. St. Paul's is very lovely indeed, but nowadays it is quite dwarfed by the modern monstrosities which overwhelm it on every side. And another peculiar thing is that nowadays they seem only to build to pull down again. Furthermore, you cannot help remembering that St. Paul's is getting on to its third century. Thinking of that, you go and sit on a bench in a little square. It is an attempt to preserve something of nature in the midst of the steel and concrete which so fittingly enclose this civilisation. Maybe there is a statue in the square, a statue of some aristocratic nonentity who happened to own the spot and so gave it his name. There he is, in the centre of the square, and as you look at him you notice that he is dressed in Roman clothes. And then it comes suddenly to your mind that those old Romans built magnificently. And not only the Romans but the Greeks. And they built so beautifully that even to this day their buildings are things of wonder and delight. Along the Embankment you will see Cleopatra's Needle. The Egyptians way back at the very dawn of the historic period built in a way that modern people, with all the experience they have had, have done little to surpass. The moderns are more ingenious, they build more comfortably, they have more of this and that and a thousand other things. But take any good history book,

and look at the illustrations and study the
dimensions of the Temple of Karnak or the
pyramids, all those thousands and thousands of
years ago. Think then of all the powers which
the slow accumulation of centuries has put into
the hands of men. Then you walk along the
streets of London again and look at the
buildings. Maybe according to the individual a
greater or smaller impression may be made. I
confess frankly that the impression which I had
at first dwindled surprisingly.

After a time, as I got my bearings, I began
to look more closely as far as previous reading,
present reading and conversation could teach
me, at what was specifically English in all this,
trying to find out, as far as I could, the particular
quality of the English people. It is unfortunate
that in the two things in which the English stand
so high, the writing of poetry and political
genius, it is unfortunate that I knew these things
before I came. The result is that I took these,
so to speak, for granted. Otherwise they would
have weighed far more heavily with me in these
instinctive impressions which I here record.
Take those two away and England suffers if you
move about London with your eyes open. There
are fine galleries of paintings. But the paintings

there, the great paintings, are not by Englishmen. You go to the concert halls. But the music is by Bach, Beethoven, Mozart and Debussy. In one respect, if you get in contact with the English people you find them a people with a quality that I think it is hardly possible for any others to surpass: love of the beauties of nature, of gardens, of flowers, of the countryside. An Englishman is as truly a poet and a connoisseur of these things as it is possible for any human being to be. You find it in the highest as well as in the lowest, a feeling as deep, as true, and as genuine in the most commonplace cockney as in the artist, the poet or the musician.

Which brings us more directly up against the object of the original quest which I have set myself—the quality of the people—the original quality of the people. It is a difficult question, a very difficult question indeed. I think I have found the answer, but it took me some time to find it and I didn't find it in London, though I have no doubt that it is there also. At first I was woefully disappointed. I listened in on the radio to famous men. I had heard some of them on gramophone records. I saw them on the screen delivering speeches. I read their utterances from day to day on political topics. Better still, I got into contact with people who had met some of them. The great political figures. The men whose names are household words. To read them is one thing. To hear them is another. It is only now that I can thoroughly understand the scorn of Swift's *Gulliver's Travels,* the amused contempt of Mr. Arnold Bennett, the delight Mr. Bernard Shaw takes in twiddling his thumbs at the whole show, the impatience of Mr. Wells, the deliberate avoidance of public life and the banging of the big drums, etc. etc., which distinguish some of the best minds of today. This question stretches out into infinity. There is so much more in it than can be dealt with in an article. There are so many things one will have to master before one can make a weighty pronouncement. Perhaps the best thing would be to leave it where Mr. Hannen Swaffer leaves it. Mr. Swaffer is not profound. He is a bit of a clown, but he has force and originality. Writing in the *Daily Herald* one day, he made a statement the truth of which I realise with every succeeding day. He said that the ordinary working man at a distance from these things is apt to be impressed by all he reads, and to believe that great and important events are being handled by necessity by great and important men. But, says Mr. Swaffer, "Go into the House of Commons, and listen to one of the great men. The chances are that he is reading the speech, and reading it badly." And not only in politics but in every other sphere. Modern journalism makes everything up to be so much greater than it really is. And as for actual achievement! For six months they have been discussing disarmament. They have achieved absolutely nothing, not one single thing. The Lausanne Conference, another fiasco. The Ottawa Conference, nothing to speak of. They do nothing and they do it badly. When one reads of the work of men like Trotsky, Lenin, Mussolini, Mustapha Kemal, one is amazed at the futility of most of the big men in English public life. France is equally bankrupt. Germany oscillates between a feudal baron like von Papen and a cinema gangster like Hitler. And as for that dreadful country America. Western Europe can say at least that she is better off than America—if that is any comfort.

Leave the big men. Come to the rank and file, the everyday person. Londoners have had sixty years of compulsory education and all the advantages of a great modern city. When you look around at the intellectual quality of the people you are astonished. I can well imagine the wrath of people who are ridden by phrases at my rashness and my impatience. I give the reader the facts and let him judge for himself. Let the stranger leave his house on a Sunday morning and go out into the London streets. Newspapers are being pressed on him from every side. What do these newspapers contain? In the majority of them there may be half a column on disarmament, half a column on the European situation, half a column, no more, and that written in the most superficial style, on any question of the gravest civic or international importance. He will, however, be able to get columns and columns on how many wickets Tate took and how many runs Hobbs scored. It is a matter obviously of the most desperate importance whether Paynter will go to Australia, or whether Alex James will be sufficiently recovered to play in the Cup Final. Austin's chances of beating Vines are the subject of learned and minute investigation, while the arrival or departure of a film star from America is noted as a hundred years ago the arrival or departure of Wellington would have been announced. That, however, is the lesser part of the Sunday fare. That by itself is the sauce. The real basis of the Sunday intellectual meal is the stories with a crime or sex interest.

No one who has not experienced it can ever understand what the atmosphere of the Sunday reading is like. Let me give as imperfectly as I am able an impression of one Sunday's newspapers. Open one newspaper. The *pièce de résistance*, placarded on every hoarding, is an account of Mrs. Barney herself of her home life, with the man for whose murder she was tried, four or five columns. Open another paper. There you will read four or five columns of what purports to be the diary of the murdered man which he miraculously had sent to the newspaper just a few days before he was killed. Open another paper. There, as the leading feature for that day, are articles by the Rector of Stiffkey's wife and the Rector of Stiffkey's daughter on what they think of the Rector and the sordid life that unfortunate old man has led during the past few years. Yet another paper tells you of June's marriage with Lord Inverclyde and promises to tell you next week of her honeymoon with the divorced lord. It is written by June herself. What could be more exciting than an account of a honeymoon by the bride herself? Yet another paper has an article on Dangerous Women by Harold Dearden. It is time I stopped. But when you stand up before a newsagent's and see all these papers advertising, each as boldly as it can, what at great trouble and expense it has provided for millions and millions of readers, you are amazed. Far better the *Port of Spain Gazette* than any of these products of a great civilisation. I write that and mean it in the most honest and sober sense of the words. Nor am I alone. When you talk to thoughtful people here they are as aware of it as any stranger and at times they are so incensed that they protest. The article by Mrs. Barney aroused such violent protests that it was withdrawn. But every Sunday morning will give you its like. All popular papers give it. The only inference is that if they do not give it they are doomed. Neither have I space to refer to the series of reconstructions and reminiscences of murders and other similar phenomena by Sir Bernard Spilsbury, by the ex-detective and the other ex-chief of police, etc., etc. Sunday is the only day they have to read and that is what they want.

Mind you, there is an English culture, there are people who live a life of high civilisation, there are many fine and extremely able people. But in the same way as in a small island like ours you will get men thrown up every now and then, men of exceptional talents, so where you have millions and the rewards are so much greater, the opportunities of advancement so numerous, in proportion you will find a certain number of unusually gifted persons. Maybe the real test of any civilisation is the number of such persons. That, alas, is another huge and difficult question. But the average Londoner, judging him by the indications which I have given and others which I have not the time to give, has not impressed me. Nor for that matter does he impress the clear observers of his own race. What the average Frenchman or the average German is, or rather I should say what their general level is, I do not know. I hope to know in time. But at least the reader will understand, if he does not agree with, my views.

It is not that I am unaware of the vast complexity of modern civilised life, and the great improvements in sanitation, the triumphs of modern medicine, the marvellous mechanical developments of the modern age. But I ask myself what in the name of heaven is the use of a newspaper press being able to turn out 168,000 copies an hour if it is only printing the rubbish that it does? Furthermore, I cannot help thinking, as I look around, of the history of the English. At the beginning of the Christian Era they were quite wild and savage. The Romans spent four hundred years here, four hundred— a period about as long as from the discovery of America to the present. Yet as soon as they left the inhabitants slipped back into barbarism again. After a century or two, Roman civilisation again came, through the church. And in 1066, through the Normans, again there was an influx of a high civilisation. Since then they have had nearly a thousand years of uninterrupted opportunity. Santayana says that the northern races are still spiritually immature. The difference between spiritual and mental immaturity I do not know. But it does seem to me that millions of these people are still mentally adolescent. They live on cheap films and cheap newspapers.

But to find out something of what the English people are really like, of what distinguishes them, apart from increased opportunities and older civilisation, from our people at home, I had to find out not in London but in a little town in the north of England, where I am staying at present, a little town called Nelson. Nelson is a provincial town, nothing to write home about, and San Fernando, making the necessary allowances, would compare very favourably with it in many respects. But one day I got into conversation with a quite ordinary person who told me the following story.

In Nelson a few years ago there were three or four talking-picture houses run by men who were strangers to the town. The Nelson people are very fond of the cinema. They flock to it in their thousands. For many, apart from the beauties of nature, an abiding love of the English people, the cinema is the only recreation. The Nelson operators, maybe not quite a dozen of them in all, got about forty-five shillings a week. They were quite unimportant persons. The owners of the theatres wanted to reduce their salaries. But Nelson is a town where most of the working people are pretty closely united. So in order to avoid trouble the owners who ran cinemas in Burnley, a much bigger town a few miles away, hit on an ingenious plan of attaining their ends. They reduced salaries in Burnley. They attempted to transfer a Nelson operator to a Burnley theatre. Naturally the pay would be the Burnley pay, and thus the salaries would be lowered. Note, please, how careful the owners had to be in such a simple matter of lowering the salary of an ordinary cinema machine operator. That, however, is but a trifle. The Nelson people got wind of the matter. There were meetings and discussions. They decided that the salaries of the cinema operators should not be lowered. Complications began. The owners insisted. One cannot be certain of the details. But what matters is that the whole town of Nelson, so to speak, went on strike. They would not go to the cinema. The pickets were put out in order to turn back those who tried to go. For days the cinemas played to empty benches. In a town of forty thousand people you could find sometimes no more than half a dozen in the theatres. The company went bankrupt, and had to leave. Whereupon local people took over and the theatres again began to be filled. It was magnificent and it was war. I confessed I was thrilled to the bone when I heard it. I could forgive England all the vulgarity and all the depressing disappointment of London for the magnificent spirit of these north country working people. As long as that is the stuff of which they are made, then indeed Britons never, never shall be slaves.

Notes

James refers in the essays to a range of persons, institutions and events which one presumes were of topical familiarity to his original audience. Many have now lapsed into varying shades of obscurity. The aim of these notes is to shed some light on these for the contemporary general reader.

I have followed the sensible rule of annotating only those references likely to trigger questions, assuming that, like me, the reader may ask, "Who is Sydney Dark?" but not "Who is D.H. Lawrence?" But when in doubt as to whether or not to annotate, I have tried to err in providing more rather than less information than may be needed.

I have also noted the exact sources of James's several literary references.

N.L.

A Visit to the Science and Art Museums

p. 3

Victoria and Albert Museum: the U.K.'s national museum of decorative arts, originally established in 1852 as the Museum of Manufactures. Five years later it was moved to South Kensington and renamed the South Kensington Museum. It was given its present name in 1899. The Victoria and Albert also houses the National Art Library.

John Ince: I have been unable to identify this individual precisely, but it is interesting to note that, according to British immigration records, there was a stowaway named John Edward Ince aboard the *M.S. Colombia,* the ship on which James travelled to the U.K. The *Colombia's* unofficial ninety-fifth passenger was a twenty-two-year-old "salesman" whose country of last permanent residence is given as "B.W. Indies". It is not inconceivable that James encountered and befriended the stowaway during the two-week voyage.

Science Museum: originating in the science collections of the Victoria and Albert Museum, the Science Museum was established as a separate institution in 1909; in 1928 it moved to its own building in South Kensington. Today it is one of three museums collectively comprising the National Museum of Science and Industry (the others are the National Railway Museum in York and the National Museum of Photography, Film and Television in Bradford).

the airplane in which Lieutenant Stanforth won the Schneider Trophy: The Schneider Trophy competition, 1913–1931, sponsored by the French industrialist Jacques Schneider, was an international seaplane race intended to stimulate technological progress. In 1931 the British team achieved its third victory in a row and won the Trophy outright. The three members of the flight team were Lt. J.N. Boothman, F.W. Long and L.S. Snaith ("Lt. Stanforth" has proved elusive); they flew the Supermarine S6B, powered by a specially designed Rolls-Royce engine. Seventeen days after the race the Supermarine set an absolute speed record of 407.5 mph. Aircraft, engine and trophy all remain on display at the Science Museum, in the Flight Gallery.

p. 4

stays: James is probably referring to the seaplane's *struts.*

the first power-driven airplane: The Wright flyer of 1903, designed and built by Wilbur and Orville Wright, was flown four times from 14 to 17 December, 1903, becoming the first powered airplane to demonstrate sustained flight under a pilot's full control. After 17 December, 1903, it was never flown again. In 1928 it was put on display at the Science Museum, where it remained until 1948, when it was transferred permanently to the Smithsonian Institution in Washington.

p. 6

Amy Johnson (1903–1941): pioneering English female aviator who set records in 1931, for her flight across Siberia to Tokyo, and in 1932 for her solo flight to Cape Town. Her earlier attempt to break the record for a solo flight to Darwin, Australia, was unsuccessful, but brought her considerable fame. She joined the Air Transport Auxiliary in 1939 and disappeared over the Thames estuary while on a flight mission in 1941.

Miss England I: speedboat built in 1927. Piloted by Major Henry Segrave, she beat *Miss America VII* in a race at Miami Beach in 1929, despite having significantly less horsepower than her rival, but failed to establish a new world record. She demonstrated that highest speed would be achieved not merely by powerful engines, but by lighter craft with greater manoeuvrability.

Sir Henry Segrave (1896–1930): military officer, racing motorist and speedboat pilot. He was the first motorist to break the 200 mph barrier, in 1929, for which accomplishment he was knighted. After his racing success with the speedboat *Miss England I*, he set a new world record in her successor *Miss England II*. On Friday 13 June, 1930, at Lake Windermere, Westmoreland, he achieved an official speed of 98.7 mph over the measured course. On the third run, however, *Miss England II*, going at about 120 mph, struck a floating log and was capsized. Segrave was killed, but his craft was salvaged. *Miss England II* went on to achieve a maximum official speed of 103.5 mph. In the original text his name is misspelled "Seagrave".

p. 7

old clock from Wells Cathedral: the clock in the north transept of Wells Cathedral was installed in the late 14th century, probably after 1386, and records show it was in continuous use from 1392. The mechanism was modified in the seventeenth century to improve its timekeeping, and again in 1742 so that it would need winding just once a day. In 1837 a new mechanism was installed and the original moved to the Cathedral undercroft; in 1884 it was transferred to the Science Museum, where it remains on display.

p. 9

Henry Ford ... making a museum: the Henry Ford Museum in Dearborn, Michigan, opened to the public in 1933. It contains a major collection of Americana, used to illustrate "the spirit of innovation and resourcefulness" in the development of the United States.

p. 12

John the Baptist: St. John the Baptist Preaching (1878).

p. 13

"In one year they sent a million fighters forth": from stanza seven of "Love Among the Ruins" (1863 version). James's punctuation is slightly inaccurate.

The Bloomsbury Atmosphere

p. 19

I have been living in London for ten weeks: James arrived at the port of Plymouth on Friday 18 March, 1932. He is described, in the immigration records, as a teacher, and his destination is given simply as "London". If his "ten weeks" is more or less accurate, he would have been writing this essay around 27 May, just over a week after the events it describes.

Bloomsbury: the area of central London, just northwest of the City, where the British Museum and the University of London are located. "Bloomsbury" of course immediately brings to mind the Bloomsbury Group of writers, artists and intellectuals who lived, worked and met here in the first few decades of the twentieth century: Virginia and Leonard Woolf, Vanessa and Clive Bell, Lytton Strachey, Duncan Grant, Saxon Sydney-Turner and others. But Bloomsbury, due to the proximity of the university and its relatively low rents, was also the students' quarter, as James says; a Bohemian district of boarding-houses, inexpensive cafés and undergraduate intellectual ferment. This latter was the Bloomsbury to which James briefly belongèd in early 1932. Though his pamphlet *The Case for West Indian Self-Government* was to be published by the Woolfs' Hogarth Press in 1933, James had no personal contact with members of the Bloomsbury Group (whose heyday, in any case, had been before the First World War).

p. 23

Jaeger: The Jaeger Sanitary Clothing Company was founded in 1884 by Lewis Tomlin, to produce undergarments designed according to the ideas of Dr. Gustav Jaeger, Professor of Zoology at the University of Stuttgart. Jaeger argued that woollen undergarments were beneficial to the wearer's health.

p. 26

Constant Lambert (1905–1951): composer, conductor and co-founder of the Vic-Wells Ballet (now the Royal Ballet), whose choral fantasy *The Rio Grande* brought him significant fame in the early 1930s. He was a friend of the Sitwells.

p. 29

"If thou must love me": Sonnets from the Portuguese, 14. James misquotes the first line, writing: "If thou *would'st* love me".

p. 30

"O, how shall summer's honey breath": Sonnet 65. Again James slightly misquotes: "Oh how *can* summer's honey breath".

p. 31

The Oxford historian: G.M. (George Macauley) Trevelyan (1876–1962), Regius Professor of Modern History at Cambridge from 1927 and Master of Trinity College from 1940 to 1951. He was the author of, among other books, *The History of England, English Social History, England Under the Stuarts,* and volumes on Garibaldi and Lord Grey.

p. 32

Sidney Dark (1874–1947): journalist, critic and biographer of, among others, W.S. Gilbert and H.G.Wells.

p. 33

Professor Bidez: Joseph Bidez (1867–1945), Belgian classical scholar, author of *Le Biographie d'Empédocle, La Vie de l'empereur Julien* and *Eos; ou, Platon et l'Orient,* among other books. In the original text his name is misspelled "Bidet".

John Clarke: I have been unable to identify this individual, who seems to have been a Trinidadian student.

Bloomsbury Again

p. 40

"Where'er you walk": aria from *Semele* (1743), HWV 58.

p. 41

Bumpus's: J. & E. Bumpus, booksellers of Oxford Street, 1838–1960.

p. 42

Powys Evans (1899–1981): portraitist and caricaturist.

p. 43

Mitra Sinanan (1910–1983): Trinidadian barrister and politician, was called to the Bar at Middle Temple in 1931. On his return to Trinidad he was a member of the Port of Spain City Council, 1939–1942, and a member of the Legislative Council, 1950–1961. He also defended Tubal Uriah "Buzz" Butler against charges of sedition following the 1937 oilfield riots.

p. 44

C.F. (Charles Freer) Andrews (1871–1940): Anglican priest who went to India in 1904 as a missionary. Known for his relief work and championship of the poor, he became a friend and associate of Gandhi and of Rabindranath Tagore.

p. 48

Lord Harris: George Francis Robert, Baron Harris (1810–1872), British Governor of Trinidad, 1846–1854, reformer of the colony's systems of local government and education.

p. 49

Thackeray: James's enthusiasm for *Vanity Fair* in particular was almost proverbial. In *Beyond a Boundary* he reports first reading this novel at the age of eight, and re-reading it on average every three months thereafter.

p. 50

Flecker's Hassan: James Elroy Flecker (1884–1915), poet with Orientalist leanings, influenced by Wilde and Swinburne. His play *Hassan* was published posthumously in 1922.

Gilbert Frankau (1884–1952): poet and best-selling author of the novel *World Without End* (1943).

p. 51

Speech on his nose: from act 1, scene 4.

"Non merci" speech: from act 2, scene 7.

p. 52

"Will no one tell me what she sings": third stanza of "The Solitary Reaper", from "Memorials of a Tour in Scotland, 1803". James misquotes the penultimate line: "Some natural sorrow, *joy,* or pain".

The Houses

p. 65

Oscar Ribeiro (dates of birth and death unknown): Trinidadian businessman. His sister Elsie was the first wife of Eric Williams, first prime minister of independent Trinidad and Tobago (with whom James had a significant but ultimately stormy relationship).

p. 70

Lausanne or Geneva: at the 1932 Lausanne Conference representatives of Germany, the United Kingdom, France and Japan met to discuss the payment of the German war reparation debt. In February 1932 the League of Nations convened a disarmament conference in Geneva; it was concluded in 1937.

Rector of Stiffkey: Harold Francis Davidson (d. 1937), Anglican rector of the parish of Stiffkey in Norfolk, was thrust into notoriety in 1932 when it came to public knowledge that for years he had divided his attention between his parishioners and the showgirls and prostitutes of London's West End. The "Prostitutes' Padre" was tried for immoral conduct and defrocked, despite his claim that he merely had been providing spiritual ministry to the young women. His clerical career destroyed, Davidson became a sideshow performer on the Blackpool seafront, delivering impassioned defences of his innocence. He died in 1937, mauled by a fellow performer, a lion.

The Men

p. 81

Sir Henry Wood (1869–1944): conductor and composer, who established the London Promenade concerts (the "Proms") in 1895. His transcription of *Bach's Toccata and Fugue in D minor* for organ was remarkably popular.

Sir Landon Ronald (1873–1938): pianist, conductor and composer, who accompanied Dame Nellie Melba, conducted the Royal Albert Hall Orchestra, 1909–1914, and the Royal Scottish Orchestra, 1916–1920, and was principal of the Guildhall School of Music and Drama, 1910–1937.

Ernest Newman (1868–1959): the most celebrated English music critic of the early twentieth century, wrote for the *Sunday Times,* 1920–1958. He is best known for his monumental four-volume *Life of Richard Wagner.*

Frederick Lamond (1868–1948): Scottish pianist and composer, pupil of Liszt, best known for his Beethoven performances.

p. 82

William Burslem (dates of birth and death unknown): principal of Queen's Royal College in Port of Spain, c. 1910. In *Beyond a Boundary* James describes him as "part Pickwick, part Dr. Johnson, part Samuel Smiles . . . an Englishman of the nineteenth century . . . no more devoted, conscientious and self-sacrificing official ever worked in the colonies."

The Women

p. 98

twenty-five shillings a week: this sum in 1932 was the approximate equivalent of £71 in 2001, according to data provided by Economic History Services (www.eh.net).

p. 100

"a girl has got to meet the men": from the short story "Brickdust Row": "I live in Brickdust Row. They call it that because there's red dust from the bricks crumbling over everything. I've lived there for more than four years. There's no place to receive company. You can't have anybody come to your room. What else is there to do? A girl has got to meet the men, hasn't she?" James slightly misquotes the sentence: "a girl has got to meet the *man*".

p. 105

as Rosalind says, new matter: from *As You Like It,* act 4, scene 1: "Then she puts you to entreaty, and there begins new matter."

two hundred pounds a year: in 1932, the approximate equivalent of £11,450 in 2001, according to data provided by Economic History Services (www.eh.net).

p. 107

the article on Barbados: "Barbados and Barbadians" was published in the *Port of Spain Gazette* in two instalments on 20 and 22 March, 1932. It describes James's activities during the week he spent on that island (Sunday 28 February to Sunday 5 March) on his journey from Trinidad to the United Kingdom.

The Nucleus of a Great Civilisation

p. 113

a statue of some aristocratic nonentity: James may have in mind the statue of the fifth Duke of Bedford in Russell Square, situated just behind the British Museum in Bloomsbury. This district of London, which still belongs to the Bedford Estate, was developed in the late eighteenth and early nineteenth centuries.

Cleopatra's Needle: one of a pair of obelisks originally erected at Heliopolis, c. 1475 BC, by Thutmose III. In 12 BC they were removed to Alexandria by Augustus Caesar. They were moved once again in 1878, one to the Thames Embankment in London and the other to Central Park in New York. They have no known historical connection with Cleopatra.

p. 116

Hannen Swaffer (1879–1962): journalist, probably best known for defining freedom of the press as "freedom to print such of the proprietor's prejudices as the advertisers don't object to."

p. 117

Lausanne: see note to p.70.

Ottawa Conference: held in 1932 to discuss economic problems affecting the United Kingdom and its Dominions as a result of the Depression.

Franz von Papen (1879–1969): German right-wing politician and diplomat, chancellor for six months in 1932. He forced President Hindenburg to appoint Hitler to the chancellorship the following year.

p. 118

Maurice Tate (1895–1956): cricketer, an accomplished fast-medium bowler who played for Sussex and for England in 39 Test matches, 1924–1935. He took a total of 155 Test wickets.

Sir John "Jack" Hobbs (1882–1963): cricketer, considered the sport's greatest batsman between W.G. Grace and Donald Bradman. He played for Surrey and for England in 61 Test matches, 1907–1934, scoring 197 centuries over the course of his career, and was the first cricketer to be knighted.

Edward Paynter (1901–1978): cricketer, a nimble batsman and thought to be the best outfield of his day. He played for Lancashire and for England in 20 Test matches, 1931–1939. He did indeed go to Australia, for the 1932–1933 Ashes tour. Before the 4th Test at Brisbane he was taken ill with tonsillitis and eventually hospitalised; hearing that England were in difficulty, he returned to the game from his hospital bed to make 83 runs. England won the match.

Alex James (1901–1953): Scottish football player who reached the peak of his career playing for Arsenal, 1929–1937, winning the F.A .Cup twice and the Premier League four times. He missed the 1932 Cup Final against Newcastle, due to injury; Arsenal lost, 2–1.

Henry "Bunny" Austen (1906–1999): English tennis player, ranked second in the world in 1931, twice a

Wimbledon singles finalist. He lost the Wimbledon final to Ellsworth Vines in 1932. He was the first player to wear shorts on the court, in this same year.

Henry Ellsworth Vines (1911–1994): American tennis player, ranked first in the world in 1932, known for his extremely fast serve. He won the U.S. title in 1931 and 1932, and the Wimbledon title in 1932, in a furious final match against Bunny Austin (6–4, 6–2, 6–0). He lost both titles the following year.

p. 119

Mrs. Barney: Elvira Barney (1905–1936): wealthy socialite divorced from an American husband, was implicated in the May 1932 death of Michael Scott Stephen. After a night out at the Café de Paris, Barney returned with Stephen to her flat, where the young man was shot in the chest at close range. Barney claimed this was an accident that occurred during a quarrel. Despite apparently sound evidence she was acquitted. Four years later she was found dead in a Paris hotel room.

Rector of Stiffkey: see note to p.70.

June's marriage with Lord Inverclyde: the actress and music-hall performer June Tripp was married to Alan, fourth Baron Inverclyde, in 1932.

p. 120

Dr. Harold Dearden (1883–1962): writer and psychologist who in the 1920s and 30s published popular newspaper series on topics such as "Great Unsolved Crimes".

Sir Bernard Spilsbury (1877–1947): forensic pathologist, a pioneer in his field and the most eminent forensic scientist of his day. It was said that "He could achieve single-handed all the legal consequences of homicide—arrest, prosecution, conviction and final post-mortem—requiring only the brief assistance of the hangman" (Dr. Richard Gordon).

p. 122

"the northern races are still spiritually immature": it has proved impossible to identify a precise reference. A recurring theme in the writings of the Spanish-American philosopher George Santayana (1863–1952) is the contrast between the spiritual and ethical values of "Protestant" northern Europe and those of the "Catholic" or "pagan" south.

p. 123

Nelson: a Lancashire borough situated three miles northeast of Burnley and about twenty-five miles north of Manchester. Its chief industries were coal mining and textile manufacture. In June 1932 James left London to stay here with his close friend Learie Constantine, who was then playing for Nelson in the Lancashire Cricket League.

forty-five shillings: in 1932, the approximate equivalent of £128 in 2001, according to data provided by Economic History Services (www.eh.net).

Index

References to the notes are indicated by "n".

Ambard, Andre P.T., x
Andrews, Charles Freer, 44; *n* 132
Austen, Henry, 118; *n* 137

Barney, Elvira, 119, 120; *n* 138
Barrett Browning, Elizabeth, *Sonnets from the Portuguese*, 29; *n* 130
Bennett, Arnold, 116
Bennett, Louise, xv
Beyond a Boundary, ix, xvi, xxv-xxvii, xxx; *n* 132
Bidez, Joseph, 33; *n* 131
Bloomsbury, 19–54
Browning, Robert; "Love Among the Ruins" quoted by James, 13–14; *n* 129
Bumpus, J. & E., booksellers, 41–42; *n* 132
Burnley (town in Lancashire), cinema strike in, 123–125; *n* 139
Burslem, William, xvii, 82–83; *n* 135

Cipriani, Arthur Andrew, xxvii
Clarke, John, 33–34, 43; *n* 131
Colombia, M.S., James travels to United Kingdom on, xiv, xxx
Constantine, Learie, encourages James to travel to United Kingdom, xxx–xxxi; political conversations with James, xxvii

Dark, Sidney, 32; *n* 131
Davidson, Rev. Harold Francis, 70, 119; *n* 134
de la Mare, Walter, 32
Dearden, Harold, 120; *n* 138
Dickens, Charles, *The Pickwick Papers*, 49–50

Evans, Powys, 42; *n* 132

Faulkner, William, 25
Flecker, James Elroy, *Hassan,* 50; *n* 133
Ford, Henry, 9; *n* 129
Frankau, Gilbert, 50–51; *n* 133

Geneva Conference, 70; *n* 133

Handel, George Frederick; "Where'er you walk", 40; *n* 131
Harris, Lord, 48; *n* 132
Henry, O., "Brickdust Row" quoted by James, 100; *n* 135
Hitler, Adolf, 117
Hobbs, John, 118; *n* 137

Ince, John, 3; *n* 126
Inverclyde, Lord, marriage to June Tripp, 119; *n* 138

Jaeger Company, 23–24; *n* 130
James, Alex, 118; *n* 137
James, Cyril Lionel Robert (C.L.R.), attends Sitwell lecture at Student Movement House, 20–32; contrasts Bloomsbury life with "real" life, 52–54; departs Trinidad for United Kingdom, xiii–xiv, xxx; describes "types" of London women, 93–102; describes conversations with Bloomsbury friends, 39–52; describes four days in Bloomsbury, 19–52; describes Nelson cinema strike, 123–125; describes typical boarding-house, 59–66; dines with president of Society for International Studies, 44–47; discusses colour prejudice, 83–88, 102–107; education and intellectual development, xxv–xxvii; encounters Rodin's *John the Baptist Preaching,* 12–14; leaves London for Nelson, xxxi; meets businessman in Russell Square tube café, 78–81; meets Edith Sitwell, 31–32; not impressed by London, 111–122; opinions on poetry, 27–31; visits Science Museum, 3–9; visits Victoria and Albert Museum, 11–14; writes for Port of Spain

James, Cyril Lionel Robert (C.L.R.) *continued*
    Gazette, xiv, xxxi–xxxii. *See also Beyond a Boundary,*
    Life of Captain Cipriani, Minty Alley, "Triumph"
James, Juanita, xiv
Johnson, Amy, 6; *n* 128

Keats, John, 27–30
Kemal, Mustapha, 117

Lambert Constant, 25–27; *n* 130
Lamming, George, *The Pleasures of Exile,* xv
Lamond, Frederick, 81; *n* 134
Lausanne Conference, 70, 117; *n* 133–134
Lawrence, D.H., 23–24; *n* 97
Lenin, Vladimir Ilyich, 117
Life of Captain Cipriani, xxvii
Locke, John, 41–42

Magdalena, M.S., James travels to Barbados on, xiii, xxx
Minty Alley, xxiii
Miss England I, 6–7, 9; *n* 128
Mussolini, Benito, 117

Nelson (town in Lancashire), xxviii–xxix; cinema strike
    in, 123–125; James joins Constantine family in,
    xxxi; *n* 139
Newman, Ernest, 81; *n* 134

Ottawa Conference, 117; *n* 137

Paynter, Edward, 118; *n* 137
Philip, Michel Maxwell, *Emmanuel Appadocca,* xxvi–xxvii
Pirandello, Luigi; *Six Characters in Search of an Author,*
    48, 52
Port of Spain Gazette, compared to British newspapers,
    120; London essays published in, x, xiv, xxx–xxxii

Queen's Royal College (Q.R.C.), xiii, xvi, xxv–xxvi

Rector of Stiffkey, *see* Davidson, Harold Francis

Rhys, Jean, *Voyage in the Dark*, xvi, xviii

Ribeiro, Oscar, 65; *n* 133

Rodin, Auguste, *St. John the Baptist Preaching*, xii, 12–14; *n* 129

Ronald, Landon, 81; *n* 134

Rostand, Edmund, *Cyrano de Bergerac*, 51; *n* 133

Santayana, George, 122; *n* 139

Schnabel, Arthur, 11

Schneider Trophy, 3; *n* 127

Science Museum, xi–xii, 3–9; *n* 127

Segrave, Sir Henry, 6–7, 9; *n* 128

Selvon, Samuel, *The Lonely Londoners*, xv

Shakespeare, William, *As You Like It* quoted by James, 105; *n* 135; Sonnet 65 quoted by James, 27–30; *n* 131

Shaw, Bernard, 116

Sinanan, Mitra, 43; *n* 132

Sitwell, Edith, xvii, 20, 39, 40; appearance at Student Movement House Lecture, 22–23; conversation with James, 31–32; eccentric reputation of, 21–22; opinion of D.H. Lawrence, 23–24; opinions on poetry, 27–30; tells Lytton Strachey anecdote, 25–27

Spilsbury, Bernard, 120; *n* 138

Stanforth, Lieutenant, 3; *n* 127

Strachey, Lytton, 25–26

Student Movement House, 20–21, 39

Swaffer, Hannen, 116–117; *n* 136

Swift, Jonathan, *Gulliver's Travels*, 116

Tate, Maurice, 118; *n* 137

Thackeray, William Makepeace, 49; *n* 132

Trevelyan, George Macauley, *n* 131

Trinidad (magazine), xxvi

Tripp, June, marriage to Lord Inverclyde, 119; *n* 138

"Triumph", xix–xx, xxvi

Trotsky, Leon, 117

Victoria and Albert Museum, xii, 3, 11–14; *n* 126
Vines, Henry Ellsworth, 118; *n* 138
von Papen, Franz, 117; *n* 137

Webb, Beatrice, 33–34
Webb, Constance, xiv, xviii, xxiii–xxiv
Wells Cathedral clock, xi–xii, 7; *n* 128–129
Wood, Henry, 81; *n* 134
Wordsworth, William, "The Solitary Reaper" quoted by
    James, 52–53; *n* 133
Wright, Wilbur and Orville, 4–5; *n* 127